PRAISE FOR *LETTING GO*

'A practical and heartfelt guide to healing for anyone
who has suffered from low self-esteem, a lack of
confidence, or disordered eating. Woolf writes with
intelligence, wisdom and compassion for a generation
of women battling an enduring media onslaught
of perfectionism. The fightback continues.'

Rhiannon Lucy Cosslett, *The Vagenda*

'Psychology, philosophy and personal growth marvellously
rolled into one, *Letting Go* is a must-read. This book
shows us how to develop inner confidence, open new
doors, and rediscover joy and meaning in our lives.'

**Deanne Jade, psychologist and founder of the National
Centre For Eating Disorders**

'*Letting Go* is not about giving up, but about letting
freedom in. This brave and personal account shows us
that the path to true liberation is through embracing our
true selves, however flawed we fear they might be.'

**Sally Brampton, author of *Shoot the Damn Dog* and
columnist for *Top Santé* and *Psychologies***

'A timely reminder that though we may take ourselves
for granted at times, self-care is a divine responsibility. In
Woolf's intimately personal yet relatable voice, *Letting Go*
empowers us to accept both the role of wounded and healer.'

'Gutsy and engaging, *Letting Go* combines research and real-life advice on fulfilling your inner potential and building self-belief... Woolf's latest book is highly recommended.'
Tim Weeks, Olympic trainer

'Emma Woolf is the voice of friendly sanity; she is the warm, assured hand that reaches out and grasps yours. A wonderfully helpful book.'
Kate Long, author of *The Bad Mother's Handbook*

'Emma Woolf's book is a reminder to us all to focus on what is important in our lives; our own well-being, the loved ones around us and the community. With the pervasive technology that so often consumes us and bombards us with trivia, it is easy to forget this. The book underscores the need to reclaim a break.'
Tanya Schevitz, spokesperson for Reboot's National Day of Unplugging www.nationaldayofunplugging.com

'What an entertaining, insightful, authentic and inviting exploration into the power of letting go this book is. These words will help many people really live again.'
John C. Parkin, author of the *F**k It* books

PRAISE FOR *AN APPLE A DAY*

'*An Apple a Day* is the single most important book in my library. I genuinely believe that I am alive because of it. It saved my life.'
Martha Greengrass

'I read *An Apple a Day*, and cried and cried. Reading about the illness in black and white forced me to admit to myself that I did have a problem... Through baring your innermost thoughts and feelings you have given me so much support. Thank you.'

Tessa

'I don't think I will ever be able to find the words to appropriately express my gratitude to you for writing *An Apple a Day*.'

TJ

'I cannot thank you enough for writing *An Apple a Day*... I could write and write and write forever about all the ways you helped me, but I am going to sit and enjoy the rest of my food now, because of you :)'

Samantha

'*An Apple a Day*: inspiring and heartbreakingly honest.'

Rachel Sales, www.pinkpangea.com

'Second time reading *An Apple a Day* – honestly the most inspiring thing I've ever read.'

Charlotte (@char_cassels)

'*An Apple a Day*: I have never read anything that so accurately describes how I feel.'

Simon

'When I read *An Apple a Day*, I finally realised that my struggle was a real one and that I was not alone… Thank you for reminding me that this isn't living. Thank you for reminding me: I want my life back.'

Yasmin

'Just finished reading *An Apple a Day* – not ashamed to say I cried. @EJWoolf is a massive inspiration.'

Esther Greenwood (@amissabyss)

'I first read *An Apple a Day* when I was in my very worst struggle with anorexia, and looking back I can truly say that it was one of the things that saved me. Your words are so real and true… Opening up to the public and media about eating disorders is such an incredibly brave thing to do. I admire you so much. Thank you for everything you do.'

Aine

PRAISE FOR *THE MINISTRY OF THIN*

'Just finished reading *The Ministry of Thin* by @EJWoolf. It strengthened my resolve to be pro-cake, pro-health and pro-happiness. Awesome read.'

@CakeSpy

'I loved *The Ministry of Thin*, impressively researched and argued. It's really hard with such books to find the balance between tantrum and tirade – and you've nailed it.'

Carolyn

'It is because of you and your books that you have conveyed to me and thousands of others that I am able to truly believe I am totally, utterly, and undoubtedly worthy of being totally, utterly and beautifully free of my own demons... You have reached out to me without even knowing.'

SV

'I cannot put *The Ministry of Thin* down! It should be on school compulsory reading lists... Inspires a lot of question and debate.'

Emma Louise Vizard (@EmmiLouize)

'I'm currently reading *The Ministry of Thin* and I couldn't just let it pass by without trying to contact you and tell you how much reading it has helped me.'

Sara

'Your books *An Apple a Day* and *The Ministry of Thin* have been essential reading in preventing my own relapse while I'm studying at university. Time and again they have stopped me from falling back into that dark, dark place.'

ML

'I loved *The Ministry Of Thin* – I don't believe there's anyone with a better overall grasp of body image issues than Emma Woolf right now.'
Kate Long

'*The Ministry of Thin* is a call to arms – *Fat is a Feminist Issue* for our times.'
Katharine Quarmby, *Newsweek Europe*

PRAISE FOR *WAYS OF ESCAPE*

'Is there anything Emma Woolf can't accomplish? She has proved herself as a topical, insightful journalist, a vulnerable biographer in *An Apple a Day* and a powerful voice of feminism in *The Ministry of Thin...*'
Esther Dark, Amazon review

letting go

HOW TO **HEAL** YOUR HURT, **LOVE** YOUR BODY AND **TRANSFORM** YOUR LIFE

EMMA WOOLF

summersdale

LETTING GO

Summersdale Publishers Ltd
46 West Street
Chichester
West Sussex
PO19 1RP
UK

www.summersdale.com

Printed and bound by CPI Group (UK) Ltd, Croydon, CR0 4YY

ISBN: 978-1-84953-610-3

Substantial discounts on bulk quantities of Summersdale books are available to corporations, professional associations and other organisations. For details contact Nicky Douglas by telephone: +44 (0) 1243 756902, fax: +44 (0) 1243 786300 or email: nicky@ summersdale.com.

To Cecil and Jean Woolf

In the end these things
matter most:
How well did you love?
How fully did you live?
How deeply did you let go?

Buddha

ABOUT THE AUTHOR

Emma Woolf is a writer and journalist. Born and brought up in London, she studied English at Oxford University. She worked in publishing for ten years before going freelance, and now writes for *The Times*, *The Independent*, *The Sunday Telegraph*, *The Guardian*, *The Mail on Sunday*, *Vanity Fair*, *Cosmopolitan*, *Harper's Bazaar*, *Grazia*, *Red*, *Psychologies*, *Top Santé* and *The Sun*, among others. Media appearances include *Newsnight*, *Woman's Hour*, *World at One*, *PM* and Radio Five Live. Emma is a regular on Radio 4's *Saturday Review*, BBC London's *Review the Day*, and BBC Radio Ulster. She's also the co-presenter on Channel 4's *Supersize vs Superskinny*, and has been twice nominated for Mind's Journalist of the Year award.

Emma is the great-niece of Virginia Woolf. Her non-fiction includes the bestselling *An Apple a Day* (2012) and *The Ministry of Thin* (2013). Her first novel *Ways of Escape* was published in 2014.

You can follow Emma on Twitter @EJWoolf.

ACKNOWLEDGEMENTS

Thanks to everyone who has kept me going during the writing of this book. Particular thanks are due to the following:

Everyone at Summersdale Publishers, especially Alastair Williams, Claire Plimmer and Lizzie Curtin; and Abbie Headon and Debbie Chapman for their patience, editorial insight and friendship. Thanks to Emily Kearns for copy-editing, and Marianne Thompson for the cover design. Thanks to James and Sarah Roy, and Kate Hewett, for a truly transformational retreat.

Thanks to some special friends: Joanna Tarbit, Darren Bird, Nick Breakell, Michael Lee Rattigan, Libby Courtice, Rita Guenigault, Susan Archer, Ilya Fisher, Mark Walsh, Fran Twinn and Beth Wilson.

Thanks to my inspiring readers: far too many to mention by name, but you're the most important people in this business.

Thanks also to everyone on Twitter for endless amusement and distraction.

To TGW, Marie Schendler, and Nana, in loving memory.

Thank you to my amazing siblings, Katie, Philip, Alice and Trim, and to my parents Cecil and Jean Woolf… 'It is not words could pay you what I owe.'

CONTENTS

Introduction

*Some of us think holding on makes us
strong but sometimes it is letting go.*

Hermann Hesse

I still remember the moment I realised it was time to let go. I was coming to the end of a mind-body-spirit retreat in France. I'd had no contact with the outside world for nine days, so I was feeling uncharacteristically peaceful.

On the final evening I wandered down to the river alone. Sitting there in the dusk, a single line kept running through my head: *Don't try to hold back the river*. It was something I kept hearing on the retreat: *Look at the way water flows over the riverbed. Let your life flow as naturally and easily as water… don't try to hold back the river*. Watching the water flowing smoothly around rocks and pebbles, never stopping for obstructions, just flowing on, I found myself close to tears.

I knew, with absolute certainty, that it was time to let go. Happiness was within reach, but I needed to flow around the rocks and pebbles in my path, rather than getting stuck on them. Consciously or not, I'd been holding myself back for far too long. But could I do it? Could I leave the past behind, relinquish control and allow my life to flow as naturally as water?

I sat beside the river until night had fallen. In the darkness I could no longer see the fast-flowing waters, but I could still hear them. I was filled with jittery emotions of relief, excitement and unease. Change and uncertainty were my greatest fears, now it was time to face them head on. I was making a conscious decision to let go. Along with relief, I also felt empty... Anxiety and struggle were my *modus operandi*: what would life be like without them?

OK, I needed to let go: that was clear. But what, really, was I letting go of?

I was letting go of a badly broken heart, and a legacy of grief and bereavement which I had never faced. I was letting go of a decade of anorexia, with all the confusion and isolation that had brought with it. I was letting go of shame and despair; I was letting go of hope. That sounds defeatist, but it wasn't. Until I stopped hoping to change my past, or change other people, I couldn't move forward.

Many of us live in the present surrounded by the past: painful memories, experiences or conversations, difficult family relationships or failed love affairs, emotions which have been misunderstood. We replay failures or humiliations, we repeat childhood patterns: we persist in behaviour which we know we should leave behind. I was full of all that, and more.

Sometimes you can be trying too hard. I wanted the perfect recovery: I wanted to be healthy, fit and happy. I wanted to heal everyone who was still unwell, to make them happy too. I wanted to write more and work harder and be a 'success' (whatever that means). I wanted the perfect relationship and I wanted to become a mother.

The more I tried to will everything right, the less it worked out. You know the definition of insanity (attributed to Einstein): doing the same thing over and over again and expecting different results. My life had become an embodiment of that paradox. Perhaps it was time to stop trying altogether.

It wasn't only letting go; I had to start actively changing. I had to find the bravery to try new things. After ten years in the wilderness, I had some catching up to do. Food, love, friends – by throwing off the shackles of control I was giving myself permission to live again. Getting out of that wilderness hadn't been easy: now I was free and I had to do something with that freedom. I'd gained weight and restored my health. I'd met the right man, fallen in love and we were planning to have a baby together. Everything was hopeful; anything was possible.

And yet, I was still stuck. Despite all the exhilaration of recovery, something was missing. I had learned that losing weight was not the answer to happiness – but what was? I often think of a line in the Bible, Jeremiah (17:9): 'The heart is deceitful above all things.' From the outside I was a new person, but it didn't feel like it inside. I might be recovered, but I still wasn't quite letting go.

Letting go isn't giving up: it's knowing when to move on. It's knowing how to walk away with dignity. It's refusing to allow your past to define your present or your future. It's not a state of denial, it's not pretending that bad things haven't happened, or that you're not hurt. There is a time and a place for therapy and self-reflection and learning from the past. But there is also a time to accept that some things cannot be fixed, no matter how hard you try. Some things stay broken. Some relationships have run out of steam. Some dreams need to be quietly forgotten.

I had been holding on to old hopes and dreams for too long. I kept repeating the same patterns, an exhausting ricochet between openness and wariness, confidence and despair, rejection and being rejected, retreat, privacy, floodgates open, then barriers up. I was trying to control every aspect of my life, but emotionally I was a mess. The rigid control came from a place of profound fear that if I let go, I might fail – and if I failed, I was useless. What was stopping me from simply taking a deep breath and believing in myself? What was holding me back from letting go?

Nothing was holding me back – nothing but the usual self-doubt we've all felt; those illusions we create inside our heads that others are happier or more successful. That we're somehow inadequate, insignificant or lagging behind in the life stakes. The most important lesson we can learn, from every positive and negative experience, is to keep going. No setback is ever as bad as it seems: in fact, the only failure is to give up.

We may not always feel confident, but not giving up is brave. Some days, just keeping going takes immense strength. Nothing changes unless we find the courage to change it – but we have to keep moving, learning, risking and failing, because the same old paths don't lead anywhere new. You can stay stuck for years, or you can make changes in a few days or weeks.

This book is about why I got stuck, how I got unstuck and what happened along the way. This book is about you too – about all of us: why we deserve to heal and be happy; how to forgive ourselves and others; how to love deeply, live fully and learn to let go.

Chapter One

TRANSFORMATIONAL RETREAT: LEARNING TO LET GO

'After the meditation session this evening, can you stay behind? I've noticed your breathing and I'd like to do some work on your diaphragm.' James smiled at me, removing the electrodes from my brain cap. I nodded, wondering what on earth he was talking about, and left the treatment room in silence. Moments later, rinsing off the conductive gel in the shower, I found myself close to tears. Was this the 'emotional wall' I'd heard about? What was wrong with my breathing anyway – why was he singling me out? I felt irrationally upset: if I couldn't even manage to breathe, what chance did I have of fixing everything else? So began the second day of my transformational retreat.

I had booked my place on the retreat a few months earlier during the summer, in a mood of optimistic self-improvement. A nine-day programme of neurofeedback, yoga and meditation, it seemed an interesting combination of science and spirituality.

My reason for going was simple: I was stuck. I had been fully recovered from long-term anorexia for about two years, but after all that time focusing on my physical health, I needed help healing my mind and my heart. The stronger my body grew, the more I began to see that recovery wasn't just about gaining weight. It was also about relearning how to eat with others and how to relax around food.

Most of all, I had to learn how to let go. I was tired of struggling with guilt, anxiety and control. After a decade of rigid self-discipline, perhaps it was no wonder this mindset had become so ingrained. Overcoming anorexia was the hardest thing I'd ever done and the process had taken its toll. Now I was ready to leave the shame and the sadness behind; I was ready for the next phase of my life.

Life was busy in the weeks leading up to the retreat and I had little time to focus on what was ahead. It was only at the airport that I looked at the brochures properly:

'Aimed at spiritual practitioners who wish to take a step forward in their path, this Transformational Retreat will explore the themes of nature... Using the best neurofeedback technology, yoga, meditation, bodywork and shamanic ritual, we'll shake out the old and bring in the new.'

Shamanic ritual? Bodywork? I could feel my anxiety levels rising. In retrospect, it was naïve to have signed up for this particular retreat, with its emphasis on spiritual development, something I'd always been sceptical of. In fact, I had enquired about neurofeedback sessions in their London clinic, a course of brain training without the hippyish retreat, but they were fully booked for the next six months.

I arrived at the retreat full of trepidation. Even though I wanted to feel less anxious, to commit fully to my relationship, to embrace the future; even though I knew I had been 'stuck' for too long, the idea of changing scared me too.

I'm not alone in this: we humans are creatures of habit. We remain in relationships which have gone stale, we stick with jobs or friendships that are way beyond their sell-by date. We get stuck in the comfort zone, no matter how uncomfortable it becomes. We maintain habits for which we despise ourselves – smoking, drinking, overeating – because it's easier to stay stuck than it is to change. Change means uncertainty, change demands courage. Change carries the possibility of humiliation, disappointment or failure. Not changing can be boring, but safe.

I had been repeating the same mistakes for a long time, shutting others out, avoiding commitment, building barriers. Physical intimacy was OK, but emotional intimacy made me anxious. I manned my fortress as if the barbarians were at the gate. Contemplating the future, I knew I needed to start afresh and coming on this retreat was the first step. But the possibility that I might become less tense, anxious, controlling – that I might learn how to let go of everything that was making me miserable – this was as unsettling as it was necessary.

There were six of us at Tourné, an old French manor house tucked into the Artillac forest valley on the edge of the Pyrenees. By the middle of the week, everyone was reacting differently to the treatment. One of the women had a splitting detox headache, another was sleeping incredibly deeply. One man found himself recalling strange memories, such as the names and faces of his primary school classmates from 40 years before. I was alternating between insomnia and vivid dreaming, but I felt mentally alert too: engaged and present in my body. One experience we all shared was the exhaustion: transformation would prove to be surprisingly hard work.

Although this was a group retreat, there was no group therapy – everyone arrived with their own reasons for being there and there was no obligation to 'share'. Neurofeedback is a completely individual process: we worked one-on-one with the practitioners.

The others ranged in age from mid-40s to late 50s: I was the youngest by ten years. There were four professional women – a lawyer, an accountant, an HR director, a freelance film director – and one businessman. Of the women, one felt burnt out and was looking for a change of direction in her career, another wanted to lose weight and get in shape, one was recovering from divorce and empty-nest struggles, and the film director felt she'd reached a dead end in her life. The businessman was very quiet and spent most of the time in his bedroom, asleep I assumed. Later I heard he'd been struggling with severe insomnia for years. We were all looking for some kind of transformation in our personal lives.

'In fact, the transformation has already begun. Even the fact that you're here means that something has been making you unhappy, or uncomfortable, for a long time. You've decided to come on this retreat, and it wasn't by accident: you've committed this time and money because something is really bothering you. That's a positive. The first step in changing is wanting to change.'

James was a wonderfully open-hearted Canadian; he reminded me of a friendly puppy, curious about everything. Having worked for years in the hotel business, he had a mid-life crisis and went to India to find himself, where he and Sarah met and later married. They travelled across Thailand, Nepal and Indonesia, studying Buddhism, yoga, bodywork, nutrition and holistic medicine, before discovering neurofeedback. 'With neurofeedback we achieved, in a single week, more profound personal change than we could have achieved in years of meditation and traditional Eastern techniques,' he said. They had founded Transformational Retreats to combine the latest in Western brain research with traditional healing skills.

That first evening, we sat barefoot on silk scatter cushions and oriental rugs in the large sitting room of the manor house. A few hours before, getting off the plane in Toulouse airport, we'd been strangers, a group of stressed-looking city folk, mumbling our awkward introductions. That morning I had woken to the sound of police sirens outside my flat in central London, the clanging of rubbish bins and dreary autumn rain. Already, after just a few hours at the retreat, I felt I was in a different world.

With candles and incense burning, James and Sarah told us about the week ahead. They warned us that we were likely to feel very tired: 'Your brain will be sorting and processing a lot of old stuff and forging new neural pathways.' Twelve neurofeedback sessions in nine days is an intensive programme. At their UK clinics, it's administered once a week over several months.

As well as the tiredness, we'd feel ravenous too, they said: bowls of nuts and seeds were placed throughout the house, and we were encouraged to keep our protein levels topped up. Even in a normal resting state, the brain is a 'hungry organ', consuming over 20 per cent of our daily calories – and it craves protein like crazy when it's forming all these new connections.

Food was plentiful, but incredibly healthy: platters of quinoa, brown rice, green beans tossed in garlic, avocados, ripe cherry tomatoes, lettuce and cucumber fresh from the vegetable garden. For dinner, mouth-watering soups of carrot and coriander, broccoli and Stilton, fresh pea and mint, all homemade in the old farmhouse kitchen. This is what nutritionists mean by 'eating the colours of the rainbow': everything was colourful and bursting with flavour.

Those simple meals punctuated our days. It was a shock to find myself looking forward to sitting down at the large trestle table, breaking bread together. For years, eating in public had been extremely difficult for me: even in recovery, I preferred to avoid social situations involving food. Yet there I was, eating with the others and enjoying it. Perhaps something transformational really was taking place.

Each day after lunch we had nutritional masterclasses in the kitchen, where we experimented with vegan recipes and learnt to get excited about bee pollen, chia seeds, spirulina, goji berries and raw cacao. Among the new taste experiences for me were sliced beetroots glazed in honey, and grated carrot and wakame seaweed salad – two dishes I'd never encountered before. I also ate dessert for the first time in many years, an Armenian fruit salad of melon, figs, pistachio and pine nuts. I tasted it solely because the others were saying it was delicious (and it was). Trying something just because I wanted to – this was a personal breakthrough. I was *joining in*.

The emphasis was on nutritious, unprocessed food, almost entirely vegetarian. I haven't eaten meat or fish for 15 years, so I didn't register the vegetarian aspect, but there was excitement in the ranks when chicken appeared in a lunchtime curry. A couple of the meat eaters were longing for protein and a breakaway group walked five miles into the village one afternoon for cheese supplies. Lamb was served at the 'last supper', which also caused a spontaneous overflow of joy.

The absence of meat wasn't a rule, as such, but more a way of complementing the other positive changes we were making on the retreat. There were few 'rules', but strictly no drinking was one of them. It's thought that alcohol interferes with neural pathways and, at a time when the brain is forging new connections, it makes sense to avoid alcohol completely. (We were encouraged to continue this when we returned to our old lives.) Although I missed having a glass of wine on the first few evenings, I soon started to enjoy being booze-free. The five of us women frequently complimented each other on our glowing skin and sparkling eyes, to make the abstinence easier!

While I didn't mind the lack of meat or alcohol, the lack of technology was more challenging. For me, being completely disconnected was one of the most radical aspects of the retreat. I still don't understand how something so simple could be transformative, and why I'm not able to avoid the Internet and social media of my own free will. Why does it take enforced seclusion and a costly retreat to make me disconnect?

Looking back, I see how desperately I needed to switch off. That autumn, I had been close to meltdown. It had crept up on me, a combination of writing deadlines, digital overload, too much work and too little sleep. I felt profoundly out of touch with the real world and with myself.

So I decided to make my break from technology total. We had been advised to leave laptops and tablets behind, and encouraged to keep our phones switched off. Wi-Fi was available in certain areas of the manor house, but was intermittent. The neurofeedback process is thought to be far more effective in a neutral environment. (For the same reason, couples aren't encouraged to come on these retreats, because one needs to disengage from *all that* – whatever *that* is – in order to start afresh. If you go away with a partner, they reason, it's harder to break those patterns of behaviour.)

Twenty-five years since the invention of the World Wide Web, many of us are spending hours every day online. We're either on our computer, checking our emails, chatting, tweeting, or connected in some other way. What's the first thing you do when you wake up? Or before you go to sleep? While waiting for the train? In the queue at Starbucks? If you're anything like me, you're aimlessly Googling, checking out Instagram or Twitter, bidding on eBay, adding reminders to your calendar or replying to texts. How can we expect to fiddle with these devices from morning until late into the night – admit it, many of us take our tablets or phones to bed – then switch them off and switch ourselves off too?

We only need to look around to see how new technologies are changing the way we think, communicate and behave. Many neuroscientists have speculated how this constant digital saturation – something our species is not designed to cope with – might affect the brains of future generations. In the

1970s and 1980s we had non-digital childhoods, whereas most babies and toddlers are now completely at ease interacting with tablets and smartphones. According to the American Academy of Pediatrics, children spend an average of seven hours a day on various forms of entertainment media, including televisions, computers, smartphones and other electronic devices.

You don't need to be a paediatrician or a neuroscientist to worry about the effects of prolonged digital exposure: the actress Cameron Diaz recently argued in *The Body Book*: 'We have analog bodies trying to live digital lives. Biologically we have not caught up to all this technology.' There has been particular scientific focus on the damaging effects of technology on our sleep patterns. Sleep cycles are regulated by circadian rhythms, which are regulated by light and darkness. Melatonin is a hormone produced by the pineal gland in the brain and it plays a key role in making us feel sleepy. Electronic devices, such as tablets, smartphones, laptops and TVs, emit blue light, a short-wavelength light that has been found to interfere with the production of melatonin. When we have these devices in our bedrooms we're giving our bodies and brains confusing signals, blocking the natural production of melatonin and thus interfering with our natural sleep cycles. We are artificially wakeful but simultaneously sleep-starved. No wonder many of us are left feeling distracted, anxious and unable to power down.

Necessary as it was, I found the prospect of this digital detox daunting. Back in London I'd packed a stack of books – with no Internet, mobile phone or newspapers, how would I fill my time?

I needn't have worried: a personalised daily schedule was handed out to each of us on the first evening. Almost every hour of the day was accounted for, from dawn yoga to evening meditation, by way of neurofeedback, life coaching, massage and bodywork.

Our bedrooms were what you might call spartan. Mine held a single bed, a desk and chair, and a low couch, no TV or radio, no wardrobe. I found the simple surroundings a relief. I've always rather liked the idea of living in a nun's cell (in fact I've always liked the idea of being a nun). There was no mirror in my bedroom, which didn't matter since I wore yoga pants, or shorts, or a sundress every day – I had no complicated wardrobe choices to make. I didn't use my hairdryer once and I noticed that all the women quickly abandoned make-up.

When we were free, between sessions, we were encouraged to spend time alone, in silence, 'simply resting'. This was quite a radical idea. I found it hard at first without my gadgets, no ping of texts, no 'likes' or retweets to validate my existence. Before I left I had set an email auto-reply and told myself that nine days away from work wasn't the end of the world. What could happen that was so important it needed my immediate attention? The whole point was to leave that anxiety behind.

Once I arrived, *sans* leads or chargers, and accepted that I was stranded, truly offline, without a paddle (ok, Blackberry), after a few days I began to relish it. It was liberating, not knowing and not needing to know what was going on in the world, by which I mean who was splitting up or getting back together with whom on the *Daily Mail* sidebar. I had no radio, so no economic or political updates, no arts or science documentaries, no World Service during the night.

Of course I could have borrowed someone else's laptop in an emergency. A couple of the women did keep their phones on, and they walked down to the main road to ring their husbands and children in the evening. But on day three, when the businessman offered me the use of his iPad, I shrank away in horror and went to pick raspberries in the garden. I knew that if I glanced at my emails I'd get sucked into that endless stream of replying, worrying and replying to replies. Instead I spent hours sitting on the low couch in my attic bedroom, writing – real writing, with a pen and paper. Once I got used to the strangeness of disconnection, my over-anxious, 'busy' brain began to quieten down.

At the centre of it all were the twice-daily sessions of neurofeedback. Essentially brain training, this is a powerful way to reach states of mind which lie outside our conscious control, and to break out of unwanted habitual thoughts or behaviours. Neurofeedback is non-invasive and drug-free, and uses low-resolution electromagnetic tomography to work deep areas of the brain. Sensors monitor the electrical activity from the scalp, and translate them into audio-visual form, allowing you to recognise negative patterns and convert them into healthier ones. The result is a calm, clear, focused mind, similar to that attained by meditation or mindfulness, but far more quickly.

With its *Frankenstein*-style electrodes, neurofeedback looks like something from science fiction – possibly even a bit sinister. In fact it was pioneered by NASA in the 1960s to help astronauts who were having fits when exposed to rocket fuel. Over the decades the technology has developed and there is a growing body of scientific evidence that it works.

There is no external manipulation; this is not electroconvulsive therapy. Through its own neuroplasticity, given the right cues, it appears that the brain is able to learn and change itself. Neurofeedback has been used to alleviate panic attacks, depression, binge eating, epileptic fits and trauma. In America, psychiatrists, neurologists and military medics use it to treat post-traumatic stress disorder. It has been used by yogis and monks to attain higher levels of consciousness, and by Premier League footballers, City high-flyers, poker champions and Olympic athletes to reach peak performance. Apparently even Stephen Hawking is a fan.

I had my brain mapped on the first day of the retreat and again on the last day. The neurofeedback suite was at the top of the house, just beneath my attic bedroom. That first day, James put a tight brain cap (similar to a swimming cap) on my head. He injected conductive gel into the brain cap, and connected 15 or 20 sensors via the cap to my scalp and forehead. Then he asked me to sit motionless for ten minutes, first with my eyes open, then with my eyes closed, while the sensors tracked my brainwaves.

I felt exposed, sitting there, unable to control what my brainwaves might be revealing. Was he reading my mind, my innermost thoughts, fears and hang-ups? In that way it was unlike any other therapy I'd tried; I wasn't in control of what I disclosed.

After the scan, James began to translate the data into a visual representation of my brain activity. It was instantly clear where the problems lay: my map showed alarming red spikes in theta and beta frequencies, the areas responsible for fight-or-flight, panic and danger responses. These theta and beta spikes indicated excessive subconscious activity, leading to over-analysing, hyper-alertness, a tendency to be self-critical and an inability to power down at the end of the day. These elevated fight-or-flight responses are ideal when you live in a combat zone, but I don't.

We had not discussed my 'issues' beforehand. This was a purely neurological analysis, not a psychological assessment. But I didn't need to say a word: everything I was struggling with was right there, in my brain map.

And so to treatment. Each morning, after yoga and breakfast, I'd sit in front of a large computer screen with the brain cap and sensors connected to different areas, depending on what we were working on. It seemed incongruous, being wired up to a machine in such an idyllic setting, but infinitely more calming than sitting in a laboratory or consulting room. As I focused on the flickering screen I could see the forest through the open window beyond and hear the sound of birds.

The brain-training exercises – essentially computer games – involved small coloured orbs like flying spaceships, musical waves, spinning shapes. Each person's treatment programme was individualised, to reach our optimal brain parameters. When the brain reaches the 'optimal' zone, the computer shapes move, or buzz, or flower, depending on the game. The brain likes the audio-visual feedback and wants to find that optimal state again. This is what is meant by neuroplasticity: the ability of the brain to adapt itself and forge new connections.

Eventually, given repeated positive cues, the brain shifts itself out of the old pathways, and learns to function in the new zone without prompting. You can't directly affect the images on screen so it's an odd sensation – somewhere between relaxing and focusing – and surprisingly tiring.

In the afternoons, treatment was more restful. After lunch and a life-coaching session, or bodywork, a more vigorous form of massage, I would sit in a beautiful garden room bathed in sunlight, my eyes closed, listening to vocal and musical tracks. More sensors were attached to my head, delivering electrical stimulation to specific brain regions, but all I had to do was breathe deeply and focus on what I was listening to. The tracks ranged from mindfulness exercises, to loving-kindness mantras, to intense visualisations. I started out sceptical as hell, especially when the calming, New Agey voices kicked in over the wave music, but I quickly found myself transported. Being required to sit there for 90 minutes at a time, and simply focus, my mind grew quiet. Just as in the mornings, where I found myself able to sit still for ten or 15 minutes after each yoga class, and could happily have sat there longer, in those sunlit afternoons I approached what I believe is a meditative state.

Here is a mantra from the American author and Buddhist teacher Jack Kornfield, which I was asked to repeat hundreds of times:

May I be filled with lovingkindness.
May I be safe, from inner and outer danger.
May I be well, in body and mind.
May I be happy, and free.

The words are simple but profound. Applied to one's own life, and then to others, surely this covers everything we need.

We would first spend about ten minutes repeating the mantra for ourselves. Then we were asked to picture a 'benefactor' – someone who has loved and cared for us – and repeat this phrase for them: 'May you be filled with lovingkindness.' Then we would repeat it for other people we love, for friends, for enemies, for strangers, and so on, sending the 'lovingkindness' wider and wider, until it encompasses the whole universe. With each recitation, one is expressing an intention – as Kornfield puts it, 'planting the seeds of loving wishes over and over in our heart'.

After these meditations I would walk in the garden until the sun went down, or the dinner gong rang. We ate early – this had always been a bugbear of mine – but after a few days, eating at 6.30 p.m. was absolutely fine. I walked by the river, I turned those mantras over in my mind, I savoured the silence. I had no meetings to rush back for, no voicemail to check, no emails to reply to. The digital detox for me was as therapeutic as the meditation.

Also therapeutic, in a different way, was that issue of my breathing. James had said he'd noticed my breathing was shallow, which had provoked my tearful paranoia in the shower. It wasn't abnormal to breathe shallowly, he explained: many of us breathe from the upper chest, rather than from the belly and diaphragm, because we're stressed or tense, or for no reason at all. It turned out that I had spent years taking stressed-out shallow breaths from the top of a tight chest. Breathing is something automatic, from the first lungful of air we take as a newborn. Unlike eating, speaking, even using the lavatory, no one ever teaches us how to breathe: it's just assumed we know...

James had trained with the Dalai Lama's masseur, so my breathing was in good hands. I lay on the floor of the yoga studio, on a mat, and he worked his fingers under my ribcage. He pressed up and into the diaphragm, which is attached to the underside of the ribcage, to gently stretch and loosen it. I had to breathe in as deeply as possible to fully inflate my lungs as he worked his way along each ribcage. It was uncomfortable rather than painful – and a bit awkward – but I felt the difference immediately.

Being shown how to fill my whole stomach and ribcage with air has made a real difference: my mind is calmer and my thoughts are clearer. Just as the body functions better with food, it also functions better with oxygen. Sylvain, the French bodywork practitioner, also noticed I was holding a lot of tension in my jaw, and he loosened some tight tendons around my neck and face.

For any and all our ailments, there was physical, emotional, psychological and nutritional support available. Once I got over my persecution complex about breathing incorrectly (!) it was ingenious, that James could notice something at breakfast and ask Sylvain to address it in bodywork. Another woman had persistent pain in her abdomen, and was helped in Kate's yoga classes and with Sarah's superfood smoothies. When I woke up with a rash on my face, probably a detox reaction, Sarah brewed up a compress of green leaves. Within hours, the rash was gone.

I didn't expect that from a retreat. I didn't expect anyone to care that much. The six of us lived, ate and slept alongside the practitioners in the manor house, and nothing was too much bother. I find it hard to let other people care for me; I even find statements like 'I need' hard to say out loud. On the retreat, I began to talk about my 'needs' without feeling so vulnerable.

Although we didn't divulge our personal 'issues' within the group, we often asked each other: 'So, are you feeling any better?', 'Do you feel different yet?' We'd discuss this endlessly at mealtimes, to the amusement of James, Sarah, Kate and Sylvain. I don't know what we meant by 'better', or if I felt anything changing. In neurofeedback, the brain rebalances itself without having to know what caused the problem.

James explained it to me: 'Brainwaves in proper function run like an orchestra, nothing too loud, nothing too quiet, with a harmonic beat. Neurofeedback helps restore the mind's natural balance, flexibility and harmony. Change happens in the same effortless way your body heals an injury, such as a broken rib, without any conscious direction from you. Once balance is restored, many emotional and functional conditions fall away.' Unlike talking therapies, there is no need to talk about traumatic or stressful events that triggered the problems in the first place. That's kind of unique – and a relief to someone like me, who is sick and tired of over-analysing where they're going wrong.

For all that talk of balance and harmony, it wasn't your usual pampering mind-body-spirit getaway. As the female lawyer commented, 'This is not somewhere to come and be stroked.' While the neurofeedback was fascinating and the bodywork was restorative, life-coaching was harder. I found myself coming up against difficult boundaries, and was challenged to let go of old patterns of behaviour and old emotional ties. I'd thought anorexia was the main blockage in my life – but it turned out that it wasn't the only thing I needed to leave behind. My first life-coaching session ended in tears, as I was guided through a letting-go exercise. Like my clenched jaw and tight diaphragm, I didn't expect life-coaching to be so painful.

The coaching sessions were designed to support the neurofeedback treatment, to look at what else was going on in our lives. It could be career goals, family or money-related issues, personal motivation or spiritual insights. Before my first session I had written a long wish list, but it focused on my writing, travel and work goals; nothing about emotional change, because I was fine (wasn't I?).

The truth is, I was still deeply unresolved about my last relationship. While I was happy with my current boyfriend, something stopped me from committing fully. I hadn't planned to talk about it on the retreat, but it quickly emerged as the root of all the other problems: wanting to get married, but not certain that I was ready, wanting a baby but not feeling 100 per cent sure, worrying about getting older and not having ticked the boxes, panicking about biology and fertility, comparing myself to where my mother, sisters and friends were in their 30s, feeling somehow 'left behind'.

Why couldn't I get closure on the past? My ex-boyfriend and I weren't right together, but we weren't happy apart. The level of conflict and anxiety within our relationship was impossible, but so was letting go... I wasn't sure if I wanted to spend the rest of my life with him, but I couldn't imagine building a life without him. I did not want to talk to anyone about him; I certainly didn't intend to bring it up in life-coaching.

So why did I find myself admitting that I was stuck, emotionally? That the greatest barrier to moving forward was this past relationship? I had my ambitious list of career goals: so why were we talking about him?

Paula, the life coach, asked me to picture my ex-boyfriend, and to hold him in my heart. Then she gently asked me to cut those cords, to release his image and let go with love. This was essential yet unbearably sad. I'm still working through the turmoil it has created inside.

On the fifth day, we were told to expect 'something different' that afternoon. No specifics, all very cryptic. At lunch we speculated: could this be the shamanic ritual mentioned in the brochure? Would it involve fire breathing, wild drumming, hallucinogenic drugs?

We gathered, as instructed, in the large yoga studio. Ram Chatlani sat cross-legged on the floor, and we sat around him in a semi-circle. His head was shaved, he wore flowing robes in the style of a Hare Krishna and had bare feet. I'd seen him around the grounds during the week – he owned the manor house – but so far he hadn't enlightened us, or instructed, preached, or whatever it is that a shaman does.

Despite Ram's exotic appearance, he had a cut-glass British accent, and later mentioned that he used to be a criminal barrister in London. Like James, his life had changed direction, and he had spent years exploring transcendental meditation and the Taoist arts. His 'journey of understanding' had taken him to the high deserts of Mexico where he trained with students of Carlos Castaneda.

He spoke for more than an hour on the nature of truth, the doors of perception, the search for happiness, and the meaning of existence. Then he told us we were going on a vision quest. 'Each one of you will travel alone. I want you to go into the forest and spend a few hours communing with nature. There is no goal, no agenda and no time limit. All you need for this journey is an open heart.'

OK. This was worrying. The forest was huge and mysterious, and temperatures were in the high 80s. We had been enjoying Ram's monologue – he was a fluent, inspiring speaker – but looking around the circle I could see my own panic reflected in the others. He said there were no rules and no limits to our quest: if we wanted to climb trees, or sit on the forest floor, or take our clothes off and dance, that was fine. We should allow ourselves to get lost, to follow our instincts, just to see where they led.

Telling a city dweller to 'get lost' is like telling a country dweller to navigate their way across London on the underground with a blindfold; how could I wander without purpose or direction? And no timeframe – I'd probably get bored after half an hour and then what? Could I sneak home, would he be timing us? What if I didn't have a deeply spiritual enlightenment involving dragons and fairies – could I invent something? Already I was getting anxious and trying to make this vision quest into a proper project, with objectives and clearly defined outcomes.

Wafting some incense around, Ram bade us farewell and reminded us that all we needed was our 'open hearts'. Well, that was wrong for starters. I sneaked back to my attic room, changed into my bikini and threw my sundress back on top. Then I packed a small rucksack: suncream, pen, notebook, chewing gum, sunglasses. I could be out there for hours, days

– I had no phone, what if I really got lost? What if I died of thirst? I added a bottle of water and an orange. Also I needed a towel if I was going to swim.

The idea was to let the spirit guide us, but my rucksack was bulging a bit now and the afternoon was swelteringly hot. For the first half an hour I walked straight up into the forest, along a winding track into the mountains. I didn't know where the others had gone, or where I was expected to 'lose myself': it was a narrow path, on one side a vertical rock face, on the other a sheer drop into the valley below. I could hear the rushing river below, and I grew hotter and dustier and more annoyed. I tried to get into the zone, to immerse myself in my surroundings and absorb the sounds of nature, but my conscious mind wouldn't let go. My shoulders and forehead were burning in the heat, and my jewelled sandals were killing me.

After an hour's uphill walking through the dense vegetation I reached a bend where the river joined the path. Finally I could stop, take off my ridiculous sandals and bathe my feet. But no – sitting on the rocks I saw two of my fellow questers, a few feet apart, both presumably trying to feel spiritual.

This was hopeless. How was I going to have a vision at this rate?

The further I climbed into the valley, the further I'd have to walk back down. I became fixated on the distant sound of rushing water: to hell with bathing my feet, I wanted total immersion. Ram had told us to 'follow our instincts' hadn't he? I decided to retrace my steps to the manor house and find a watering hole where I could swim. I took off my sandals, tucked my sundress into my bikini bottoms and did a U-turn. I walked as fast as the heat would allow. The stony path hurt my feet, but it was easier barefoot and I made it back down the valley in half the time.

The grounds of Tourné were extensive and there was no one around as I reached the front gate. I turned right, cut across the rambling gardens and headed down to the river – still no one in sight. I dumped my rucksack and sandals on the bank, pulled my sundress over my head and walked straight into the river.

It was shockingly cold. The river came straight from the mountain springs and was shaded by trees, so it was fresh, freezing and crystal clear. Wanting to get away from the gardens, I walked downstream, with the flow of the water, along the rocky riverbed. I reached a swathe of sunlight where the river was deeper and sat down on a large, flat rock. The water was so icy it numbed my thoughts: I slid off the rock and submerged myself completely. After the heat and frustration of the forest, and my failure to 'get lost', my mind emptied at last.

As I came up for air, my hand closed around a large stone, the size of my palm. I opened my eyes and found it was an almost perfect heart shape, smooth, light grey. I swam over to the bank and flopped down on the muddy grass just like that, no towel, arms spread in the shape of a crucifix. At that moment there was nothing I would have changed, nowhere I'd rather have been. Every cell in my body was alive, feeling the odd tickle of an ant, the blades of grass on my limbs, earth on my legs, the gentle air as the sun dried the droplets of water all over my skin. I lay there, not sleeping, not thinking, just absorbing the moment.

So that was my vision quest. I didn't hallucinate or hear mystical voices or even lose myself, but I found something far more extraordinary. I listened to my body, drawing me to the water, I washed away the sweat and dust of the forest, I let the river cleanse me and the sun restore me. I discovered contentment within myself and a heart-shaped stone, which I keep with me always.

The shamanic ritual didn't turn out the way I thought it should, but it was one of the best experiences of my life. Trauma release was another matter altogether. At breakfast on the penultimate day, Sarah told us that evening meditation would be followed by 'trauma release'. None of us had a clue what this involved.

Privately, I thought trauma release sounded thrilling. Words like this appeal to me (I'm sure Freud would have plenty to say). 'Trauma', 'scar', 'wounded', 'broken', 'damaged'; they seem to plumb the depths of pain, to encompass the world of human suffering, the hurt we all carry inside. I was full of unresolved issues – trauma release was just what I needed! I thought it would be cathartic. I would let go of all that hurt piled up in the past, and emerge fully healed and reborn.

In reality, it was awful.

We had finished meditation and remained sitting quietly on our mats. On the retreat we observed this customary silence: no talking before dawn yoga, and no talking between meditation and the evening meal. James sat down in front of the class, dressed in jeans and a crumpled linen shirt, falling easily into the lotus position. His years of 'Eastern practice' had left him sun-weathered and hippy-looking, whether in a suit or sarong.

Dusk was falling over the mountainside; Sarah lit candles and closed the huge windows of the barn, as James talked us through the principles of trauma release:

If you watch animals after a traumatic event, an attack from a predator, or a near miss with traffic, they often retreat somewhere and shake all over. Even some small children do this, but we grow out of it as adults. Tension and trauma releasing exercises (TRE) are specifically designed to release deep chronic tension from the centre of gravity of the body outward. These exercises induce neurogenic tremors to dissolve the tension pattern created as a result of traumatic events.

James explained that all of us hold stressful experiences in our bodies – the 'trauma' need not be as serious as violence, abuse or rape. It could be psychological trauma, such as bullying or humiliation; social trauma, such as divorce or job loss; or physical trauma, such as injury, a difficult birth, or the death of a friend. We can even be traumatised by witnessing events we're not directly involved in, such as robbery, parents arguing or fighting, seeing horror films or violence on TV.

So far, so good. I understood that there are sources of trauma we're not even aware of; often trauma is held too deep in the body or the mind for us to be able to process it.

The first task, James said, was to thoroughly fatigue the muscles in our legs. He asked us to jog on the spot for ten minutes, or until we were tired out. We then did various lunges, and thigh and calf stretches up against the wall. We had to repeat these exercises until our muscles were close to exhaustion.

Next it was time to release the trauma. We lay flat on our backs on the mats, heels together, allowing our legs to fall open at the knees. If you've ever had a smear test, it's basically that position. We had to find the point at which there was maximum tension in our thighs and hold it there.

What happened next makes me blush to recall, even now. First to 'go' was the woman on my right. Her legs began to quiver gradually, then more strongly, until they were shaking uncontrollably. The tremors began to travel up into her pelvis, and right up her upper body, until she was jerking and writhing barely a foot away from me.

On my left, the quiet businessman seemed to have some leg tremors going on, but he wasn't completely out of control. Further down the studio, another woman was quivering like a jelly, and the smart lawyer was on another planet. Her body was shaking wildly and she was emitting strange shrieks and moans, like someone in the throes of passion. It was completely involuntary – none of them were 'faking' it – but part of me was thinking *just get a grip, for God's sake.*

My parents wouldn't have liked it; your parents probably wouldn't have liked it. TRE is that kind of thing: the ultimate physical loss of inhibition, in public. The gasping and writhing continued, spreading like a strange Mexican wave through my classmates. James circulated around the studio, adjusting positions, checking people were OK.

I did not move an inch. My legs are strong from cycling and running, which might explain matters. (In case that sounds like boasting, I willingly admit to having pathetic upper-body strength – tell me to do 20 press-ups and I will collapse after ten.) My leg muscles weren't close to exhaustion, so maybe the whole tremor thing hadn't worked. But equally, I was horrified at what was going on around me: yet more evidence of my control-freakery, or deeply repressed trauma, or this chronic inability to let go.

Maybe I'm being hard on myself. Throughout the retreat I threw myself into everything, from shamanic ritual, to body percussion, to raw-chocolate-making, to nude massage with oils. I opened up emotionally, in life-coaching, I faced my demons and I sobbed my heart out. I surprised myself at how up-for-it-all I was, given my normally controlled personality. But trauma release was going too far. I have never come so close to walking out of any class or session in my life – I felt such scorching embarrassment – for them! Not even for me!

What made matters worse was that James kept coming and 'checking' on 'how I was getting on', as if I were in labour. Eventually, after waiting around 15 minutes for the tremors to start, I gave up. My body – traumas or not – was resolutely not about to start shaking involuntarily; I simply don't work like that. I snapped my knees back together and lay back on the yoga mat, trying to ignore the groans and wild jerking of everyone around me. These were people I liked and respected – we'd become close on the retreat – but honestly, you don't want to see your friends in such a state.

Afterwards, we filed out in silence. I went up to my attic room, threw off my yoga gear and took a long shower. I felt upset and angry with them and with myself. At dinner, a few hours later, I couldn't look anyone in the eye.

Trauma release ended up being a physical, not emotional, release of trauma – the muscles are physically shaking the shock out of the body. And we're all different. Most of the participants found it liberating; one other woman, like me, found it embarrassing. The next morning, Sarah and I talked about the horrible session and I apologised. It wasn't that I wasn't trying, I said, but I'd found it impossible. She said there was nothing to apologise for. 'Ultimately it's about letting go of control. If you're not at that stage, that's fine.' Looking back, I learnt as much about myself by failing as if I had succeeded.

On the last morning it was time for our final brain scans. The atmosphere at breakfast was like exam day: we all wanted to show 'improvement', even though we'd learnt that you can't control what your brainwaves are doing.

Trying to channel my most Zen-like state (while simultaneously trying not to elevate those anxiety spikes) I sat in the chair, brain-capped and electroded for the final time. I gazed out at the forest while James scanned my neurons. The computer then processed the data to produce various charts, graphs and brain maps.

He printed them out – and look, I've passed with flying colours! The fight-or-flight activity had disappeared almost entirely, as had the peaks of anxiety and hyper-alertness. The scans had gone from alarming reds and oranges to large patches of white, indicating zero (which is the mean/normal) and some cooler greens and blues. The difference around my left and right hemispheres and in the frontal cortex was remarkable.

I was relieved at the results, of course, but not wholly surprised. Although you can't feel your neural pathways changing, I felt different – more relaxed around others and within myself.

But after nine days of intense seclusion, I was wary about returning to the big wide world. Apart from that vision quest in the forest, I hadn't left the grounds or spoken to anyone 'outside'. I found myself wondering how nuns cope with leaving the convent. Changing into skinny jeans and heels was strange, after a week in yoga pants and bare feet. As I was packing, I noticed my stash of 'emergency' diet cokes in the corner of my bedroom. Surprisingly I hadn't touched them – and haven't drunk any since. I simply hadn't needed the daily pick-me-up I used to rely on. In the same way, and without noticing, my mind had switched from panic mode into something quieter and calmer. For the first time in years my head felt clear.

And that's how I came to find myself, on that final evening, sitting beside the river. Alone in the falling dusk with that phrase running through my head: *There's no need to hold back the river*. I began to see that the fear I felt was unnecessary. At Tourné, I was learning that life didn't need to be a struggle. I was learning that letting go can be as natural as the way water flows along the riverbed.

The organisers followed up via phone and email at three and six weeks after the retreat, and they were incredibly supportive with everything from relationship crises, to when we could start drinking alcohol again, to perfecting our bee pollen smoothies and warrior poses! It turns out we all had 'wobbles' on re-entry into our old lives: I came back to London feeling like I could take on the world – meditating on the plane, smiling serenely at the traffic delays around the airport. A few weeks later, jet-lagged from a long-haul flight, I felt frazzled and burnt out.

Six months on, how transformative has it really been? Well, those frazzled feelings are normal: neurofeedback doesn't promise miracles, and it won't erase the natural ups and downs of life. But for the first time I have strategies to cope. When sadness, anger or frustration arise, which they do, they no longer overwhelm me. I'm calmer in my interactions with others, I don't face every situation as if it were a potential conflict, and I don't find myself flipping out. I've turned into a superfood junkie, happily mixing barley grass, hemp seeds and bee pollen into my morning smoothies. I even made delicious raw chocolate for my mother's birthday (a proud moment for someone who never cooks). I no longer feel the need to punish myself with exercise, so I'm alternating my longer runs with yoga and ballet. I'm sleeping better than I have in years.

According to research, the new connections in the brain don't 'wear off' – in fact, studies indicate that they're strengthened after six to 12 months. Like any muscle, the more you use them, the stronger they become. I feel more able to cope with the future, whatever it may hold. When I walked through the airport, after the retreat, my boyfriend said: 'You look about two inches taller.'

I haven't grown two inches, but I'm walking taller. Best of all, I've learned how to breathe.

Chapter Two

CHANGE YOUR BODY LANGUAGE

Think of all the decisions we face: where to live, what to study, where to work, who to date, when to marry, whether to have children. Sometimes it can feel like we have too many options over where, how and with whom we spend our lives. But for all those choices, there's one place we can't ever leave. And that's our own body.

The remarkable thing is how little we cherish our bodies. How much we take them for granted. The muscles and bones, which enable us to walk and run; the skin, which keeps us safe and clean; the brain cells, which make it possible to think and talk and dream; the nerves, which allow us to touch and kiss and hold. All in all, our bodies are miraculous machines... and we spend so much time wishing they were different.

I'm not against physical change *per se*. There are plenty of positive improvements we can make: exercising regularly, eating fresh, healthy food, cutting down on alcohol or giving up smoking.

And there are other harmless cosmetic tweaks we can make if we want to: wearing make-up, covering grey hairs, dressing up. But, overall, we are the way we are. If we're tall or tiny, or pale skinned or dark, with a big nose or small hands – short of drastic surgical intervention, our basic characteristics are with us for life. Given that we're more or less stuck with the body we were born into, isn't it worthwhile coming to some kind of truce with it? Might it be possible, one day, even to become friends?

I received this email from my editor at the magazine *Top Santé*:

> *Hey Emma, every month we feature a few contributors at the front of the mag… For our new year issue, the question we're asking is: What's your favourite part of your body and why?*

At first I wasn't sure. I'm always preaching that we shouldn't break our bodies down into parts, or fixate on 'problem areas'. But in the end I sent this reply:

> *Favourite part of my body: my legs. Not because they're long or in any way perfect (they're not) but because they allow me to run and cycle and have adventures. My legs are strong, they look good in jeans and they carry me to the people I love.*

I truly believe in this way of thinking. During recovery, learning to value my body for what it does rather than how it looks was a game changer. I had to block out the mental anxiety over numbers on scales, weight and BMI, calories and fat, and instead focus on my physical health. Even now, in a much stronger place, I continue to make that choice. That's why I chose to 'love' my legs for *Top Santé*. I could scrutinise my thighs for signs of cellulite, I could focus on childhood scars on my knees, I could enumerate any number of imperfections, but really, what are legs for? I'm not a model, and I live in a country with rubbish weather, so what would I do with long, tanned, flawless limbs? Far more useful to have legs that perform their leggy function – and mine do, admirably.

When I was 12 or 13 years old, a girl in the school changing room commented on a vein on the back of my leg. It's behind my knee, a totally normal place to have a vein as it happens. I hadn't noticed it before, but the more I looked at it, the more paranoid I felt. I dreaded wearing shorts and skirts in the summer, solely because of this vein. As a teenager I visited my GP several times, begging to have it removed. No matter how many times he reassured me it wasn't a varicose vein – I simply had pale skin and the blue vein showed through, it didn't hurt or protrude and it didn't need surgery – I still hated it.

Over the years, I resigned myself to this evil leg vein. Mentally I put it in the 'when I win the lottery' box – if the NHS wouldn't help me, I'd deal with it when I was rich. One day, in my early 20s, I was on holiday in Greece with a boyfriend. Walking back from the beach on our final day in shorts and bikini top, happy and relaxed from a week of sunbathing, I mentioned the vein. What? He didn't know what I was talking about. We'd been together for over a year and he'd never even noticed it.

Looking back, I can remember just how paranoid I was about this vein – truly, I hated my left leg! Now I can honestly say I don't care. It's just part of me, and I'd no more change it than I'd change my left hand or my left ear. If anything, I'm quite fond of it now, the way you might feel affection for a smelly old dog or a battered but trusty car. It's a vein and it's slightly visible – so what, it carries blood around my body. And yet, for years, it made me feel ugly.

This is a bad female habit: eye-tracking software has shown that women are particularly prone to focusing on specific body parts when looking at images of other women. The same eye tracking showed that men tend to take in the whole body shape instead of fixating on specific areas. This female tendency to divide the body into parts is encouraged by tactical advertising in which we're reminded of our problematic areas – flabby arms, 'crow's feet' and 'lion wrinkles'. When women undress, we do the same thing in the mirror, fixating on the so-called 'unsightly' bits instead of the overall package.

The obsession with female body parts is rife in the media. The paparazzi lenses zoom in on bottoms, breasts and, of course, that media favourite, the celebrity 'bump'. If any female celebrity steps out holding a large handbag, wearing a baggy top, or attempts in any way to shield themselves from the flashbulbs, the wombwatch speculation begins: 'Is she? – isn't she?' Once pregnancy is confirmed, bumpwatch begins in earnest. Whether they're 'proudly displaying', 'stylishly showcasing' or 'modestly concealing' it, the scrutiny on the average celebrity pregnancy is relentless. The fact that the bump is actually a developing human baby seems irrelevant.

Then there's the insurance of celebrity body parts, which verges on farce. It has been reported that Kylie's bottom is insured for $5 million, Heidi Klum's legs for $2 million and Madonna's breasts for $2 million. The most famous body part of modern times is, of course, Kim Kardashian's bottom. Apparently she and her husband Kanye West have taken out an insurance policy for $21 million to protect her most prized asset (sorry, ass-et). A source in *Grazia* magazine in April 2014 said: 'Kanye encouraged her to take out the policy to safeguard it in the future... he got their broker to value Kim's bottom. Various factors were taken into account, including how much of her work is based on her behind and how it would be impacted if it were to be damaged.'

I've never quite understood this: what do celebrities imagine will happen to their breasts or bottom? What tragedy would have to occur for the policy to pay out these vast sums? Would one's rear end becoming droopy constitute damage? What if they stopped going to the gym and started gaining weight, would they lose their no-claims bonus?

Fortunately, most of us will never have to grapple with the small print of these bizarre body-insurance policies. There is a fine line between liking our bodies – however flawless or flawed they may be – and accepting that they're *only* bodies. Gravity will take its toll, no matter how furiously we diet or exercise. As life expectancy increases, and we're all living into our 80s and 90s, wouldn't it be great if we could appreciate mature sagginess as much as youthful perfection?

Going back to *Top Santé*'s original question, you may be curious as to what the other contributors selected as their favourite body parts. Responses ranged from 'my hair – it's super-straight' to 'my cheekbones' and 'my back and arms – when I tone up'. In all the responses there was a careful note of self-deprecation. One of the editors wrote: 'I look like a sexy animal. From the waist up anyway...' Another commented:

'I've learnt to love my strong thighs, which compensate for my puny arms.' And my response: 'My legs. Not because they're perfect (they're not)...' There's a fine line between liking one's appearance and being a show-off: it's clear that we're all wary of sounding smug, or crowing about our bodies. We all chose fairly unthreatening attributes: straight hair, strong thighs, toned back. Would any of us have dared to say 'perfect breasts' or 'pert bottom', I wonder? Would men's responses have been less apologetic, less jokey?

I asked on Twitter and Facebook what others (male and female) like about their bodies. Here are some of the responses:

* 'My favourite part would have to be my mouth... It allows me to tell the people I care about that I love them, and allows me to speak my thoughts, my beliefs and my mind.' (Lauren, 20)

* 'My hands: I don't really like the way they look but they're the only things I can truly rely on. My hands enable me to play the piano and one day I hope to practise surgery – so they're pretty important to me!' (Oliver, 20)

* 'My favourite part of me is my eyes. They allow me to see all the good and bad in the world. I would hate not to see my three-year-old son changing and growing... The joy on his face when he completes the simplest task – that to me is priceless.' (Donna, 40)

* 'For me it's all about the muscles: biceps, pecs, abs. After many hours in the gym I'm pretty ripped.' (Darren, 41)

* 'My favourite part of my body is my mouth because smiling and laughing is such a good feeling, it usually means I'm

feeling confident, and last but not least it can uplift others too! I suffered from body dysmorphic disorder for three years.' (Milly, 21)

* 'My hands – they let me do all sorts of practical things: working on the car, digging the allotment, steadying my camera, fixing my bike, etc.' (Paul, 35)

* 'My legs – they're the only part of me which reliably stay more or less the same size and shape, as the rest of me expands and contracts. Reliability, that's what I like.' (Nina, 35)

* 'I like my shoulders and my arse is quite peachy.' (Michael, 40)

* 'One of my friends is a ballerina, and she's always jealous that I have really high arches on my feet – since then they've been my favourite part. I can't change them, unlike other parts that I hate because I think they're fat. My high arches also allow me to wear high heels without being in pain!' (Christy, 19)

* 'I don't have a favourite part but I like the top half of my body. The bottom half doesn't work properly and needs constant operations. The top half is pretty good: strong arms and stomach from carrying myself around on crutches, and I've got pretty amazing eyes, if I do say so myself.' (Amber, 22)

Not a single woman said breasts. Why not? I like my breasts. Men LOVE our breasts. It's strange, what we feel able to 'like' about ourselves and what men appreciate. I wasn't surprised that I received more than 50 female responses and only five male, but I found it interesting that men mentioned their hands, their muscles, even their 'peachy' arses, whereas women focused on eyes and mouths.

There was also a physicality to the male responses I received. The men clearly saw themselves as doers, describing their bodies as practical, strong machines, which enabled them to work out or dig the garden, to play the piano or practise surgery. The female responses were more sentimental: they valued their mouths, for smiling and talking with others; their eyes, for seeing their loved ones.

That's not to say that women are weak – Jane, 36, sent me this: 'What I like about my body is that it's strong and fit. I can run for miles, I can work for hours, and I can get on the floor and play with my kids. My body has grown, carried and delivered two enormous babies and remained intact.'

What could be more powerful than a body that literally creates another human being?

Whatever we've been through, it's not always easy to find something to celebrate about our own bodies. Once it had been pointed out to me, that small vein on the back of my leg grew, in my mind, into a monstrosity. When we fixate on our perceived flaws, as I was doing, we blow them out of all proportion. It's a depressing cycle of negativity which takes the joy out of living. I avoided wearing shorts for years because of that vein – which isn't that extreme, admittedly, but it's kind of sad. However, feeling fat or ugly can have more severe consequences, undermining our self-respect, and preventing us from fulfilling our potential. It can curtail our daily activities and chip away at our professional confidence. And it saps our emotional energy: hating oneself is tiring.

I was discussing this with a 17-year-old student of mine. She said: 'If I didn't spend half the day thinking about how crap I looked, I'd have so much free time – free head space, to think about other things…'

I was sad to hear this – she's bright, talented and far from 'crap' looking – but I understood why she said it. We actually spent the rest of that session discussing what she loves and is good at, including photography, dancing and fashion, and which college courses she might apply for. Obviously self-esteem is not an issue that can be solved in a single conversation, but since then, she hasn't once mentioned looking 'crap'.

We all have 'ugly' days, but what if you feel unattractive all the time? Sadly, it seems that a growing number of us do. Surveys abound in this area, and all report a consistently high degree of body image anxiety: 77 per cent of British women hate their stomachs; 82 per cent feel that their hips are too big; 85 per cent are unhappy with their shape; 90 per cent say their appearance depresses them; 80 per cent believe their lives would 'improve considerably' if they were happy with their body.

In a survey carried out for *Glamour*, 97 per cent of respondents admitted to having severe negative thoughts about their body every single day. On average, the participants experienced 13 negative body thoughts per day – around one negative thought for every waking hour. Other surveys estimate the tally at around 36 negative thoughts per day – around 252 self-loathing thoughts per week. Is it any wonder that rates of depression in women and girls have doubled since the year 2000?

And it's not all about weight: in fact, the majority of healthy-weight (and underweight) women express the same dislike of their bodies as overweight women. The chances are that the problem isn't with your stomach, thighs or any other part of your body; it's with how you think, feel and talk about them. Here are four good reasons to ignore the ugly voice:

* It's unrealistic to pursue the perfect body and a colossal waste of time – we all have work, studies, family and hobbies, our whole lives, to be getting on with.

* It's inaccurate – the images of female beauty have often been digitally enhanced or retouched. And looking 'perfect' is a full-time occupation: celebrities and models spend a lot of time and money on personal trainers, stylists and dieticians.

* It's self-sabotaging – when we compare ourselves with others we tend to compare *up*, not *down*, which further erodes our confidence. Why measure yourself against others? Who said life was a competition?

* It's pointless – being slim and beautiful doesn't protect you against pain, illness or heartbreak. Do you really think supermodels are any happier than the rest of us?

We live in a very mixed-up society. On the one hand we inhabit these me-me-me bubbles of narcissism. We make decisions on an individual basis; we prioritise our careers, our homes, our retail desires; we expect the world to revolve around us. We want to earn more money, pay less tax, have access to the best education and health care. Compared with more collectivist societies – Israeli kibbutzim, for example, or African villages – we routinely put our own needs before those of other people.

On the other hand, we don't really like ourselves at all.

How can this be, that we focus so much time and money on ourselves, and still aren't happy with the results? As those surveys show, levels of personal dissatisfaction are higher than ever, as are eating disorders, body dysmorphia, cosmetic surgery, depression and suicide. The resources we pour into self-improvement don't make a blind bit of difference. If we're not trying another miracle diet, we're buying more therapy, or new clothes, new noses, new starts. Somehow, the selfishness doesn't translate into genuine self-respect.

We've all met those rare individuals who are happy with themselves *just as they are*. I can think of a few in my life (and I study them with awe and admiration!). My yoga teacher, Sam, is one such woman. The way she has introduced me to yoga and guided me spiritually, I can honestly say she has changed my life.

Sam is in her early 40s, a life coach as well as a yoga teacher. She's married but has no children. She's pretty and super-fit, but not flawless. She radiates calm and self-acceptance. One day after a yoga class I was helping her roll up the mats and we got talking. Imagine my surprise to hear that Sam had been close to full-on alcoholism a decade ago. That she had met her husband on an Internet-dating website. That she'd recently had a cancer scare and surgery. That they longed for children but couldn't conceive.

She told me this unexplained infertility was 'a blessing', reminding her that you can't always get what you want. Reminding her of how much she already has.

Marie is another inspiration in my life. She's in her 60s, a close friend of my mother's. She runs a guest house in Cape

Town, an assortment of bungalows scattered across a rambling leafy garden. When I was in Cape Town last year, and going through a personal crisis, mum told me to get in a cab and make my way to Marie's place. I'd never met her before, but she welcomed me like a daughter, gave me a hug and ordered me to go for a swim while she dealt with a plumber.

I ploughed up and down her little swimming pool in tears, already feeling better. Then she reappeared with a tray of toasted pitta and hummus, a bowl of grapes, and a pot of camomile tea. She wrapped me in a huge towel and we sat talking beside the pool all afternoon, our feet in the water. There was an incredible sense of peace – in the surroundings, but also within Marie.

And yet, my mother told me later, Marie has gone through hell. Decades ago her husband had walked out, leaving her with two young children. In her 50s she fell in love with another man, but he was married and hurt her very badly. She has suffered severe depression, bipolar disorder and faced countless practical struggles with making ends meet. And yet there isn't a trace of bitterness or self-pity in Marie.

I'm sharing their stories because neither Sam nor Marie is physically 'perfect': Marie has springy grey hair and plenty of wrinkles; Sam lost part of her breast to that cancer scare. They're not lucky either: their lives have been full of sadness and adversity, but they haven't allowed it to sour them. Both women are steadfast in their loyalty to others, and to themselves. We don't talk about steadfastness much these days, but it's a real gift. It means having inner resources, not being a drama queen, or blaming others, and not abandoning yourself. In her moving memoir of depression, *Shoot the Damn Dog*, the *Sunday Times* agony aunt Sally Brampton writes:

Every time you feel sad and swallow down your tears, you abandon yourself.
If somebody hurts you and you pretend you are fine, you abandon yourself.
Every time you don't eat, or fail to feed yourself, you abandon yourself.
If you don't ask for what you need when you are intimate with somebody, you abandon yourself.
If you don't ask for help when you need it, you abandon yourself.

As someone who is used to abandoning herself at the first sign of failure, these words touch me viscerally. Imagine believing in yourself, body and soul. Imagine staying with yourself no matter what happens. It's not as selfish as it sounds – accepting yourself tends to make you more accepting of others. Marie and Sam inspire me, not for their looks or lifestyles, but for their ability to be who they are. To stay with themselves when things get tough.

The Buddha says: 'If your compassion does not include yourself, it is incomplete.' It's not easy for any of us – but worth aiming for.

What has this got to do with the body, you may be thinking: surely appreciating your mind is different to appreciating your physical form? Well, they're not mutually exclusive. For a long time I thought they were: during anorexia I became profoundly disconnected from my own body. I was frightened by its appetites and suspicious of its neediness. It took a long time to understand that I could not ignore my physical needs (for food, warmth, rest) and expect my mind to be OK. Recovery meant learning to listen to my hunger as I listened to my heart. Our bodies are miraculous machines, but they need fuel to function. Don't go to war with yourself. If you don't take care of your body, you're not taking care of your mind.

Physical self-acceptance is only the beginning. As I learnt from Marie and Sam, true serenity comes from a deeper place. But feeling comfortable in our bodies would be a start. In an interview for the *Daily Mail* in April 2013, artist Tracey Emin said:

> *'I've always had a thing about my body, always not felt good about it. The happiest I am is the thinnest I can be. I think the less of me there is the better I feel about it. It's a thing you shouldn't really say, but that's the truth.'*

It's a terribly honest, but sad, thing to admit. So many of us – young or old, curvy or skinny, black or white, female or male – will identify with Emin's words. In particular her comment that: 'The happiest I am is the thinnest I can be.' If we want to change the way we feel about our bodies, we could start by improving the way we talk about them. How can we be happy *with* ourselves when we're not happy *in* ourselves?

The language of weight is loaded, of course. Words we might use about ourselves are not always acceptable when used by others. Our views will differ – is 'skinny' offensive, is 'fat' insensitive, is 'curvy' a compliment or a euphemism? There are layers of implied judgement and approval behind most of the language we use.

Think of your friends who are different sizes. How would you describe their body shapes: 'sporty', 'slender', 'hourglass'? Then think of the casual, abusive terms we use for our own bodies: 'jelly belly', 'muffin top', 'bingo wings'. Fairly light-hearted, you might think, but is it really funny? I believe the way we talk about our bodies can have a corrosive effect on the way we feel about them. So how do we approach the sensitive issue of size and shape? In our society, there is an assumption that weight loss is a good thing. It's taken for granted that we all want to be thin and that fat people hate being fat. How often do we hear: 'You're lucky to be thin' or 'She's lost loads of weight and looks great', etc. But some people hate being thin and some people like being large.

On a long-haul flight last year, I got talking to the woman next to me. Apologising for taking up half of my seat, she said she was 'too fat to fly these days'. I was flustered by her use of the F-word, but she smiled and we got talking.

'I'm fat, it's fine!' she said. 'Food is the greatest pleasure of my life. I can't imagine being thin and I wouldn't want to be. I know I'm fat and I don't have a problem with it.' She used the word 'fat' easily, without a trace of self-disgust. It was rare, and refreshing, to encounter someone who was genuinely comfortable with herself.

However straightforward the term 'fat' may be – a biological description of adipose tissue – in fact it's far from simple. In recent years 'fat' has acquired layers of emotion and frustration, judgement, blame and shame. As a society we're obsessed with weight and confused about healthy eating; surrounded by delicious (often addictive) food and ruthlessly targeted by advertisers. It's hard to find a balance amid the contradictions: on the one hand we're reminded that we're 'worth it' and encouraged to 'treat ourselves'; on the other we're bombarded with miracle diets and slimming tips, and threatened with dire warnings about obesity. It's no wonder many of us get caught up in the cycle of diet or excess, bingeing or self-denial, all or nothing.

No matter how independent or strong-minded we may think we are, few of us are immune to pressure from the diet, fitness and cosmetic surgery industries. A friend told me: 'I don't want to lose weight and I've never had a problem with my body image, but still – I hurt myself just as bad inside, constantly feeling I should have more self-discipline.'

She's not the only one to feel conflicted: our behaviours around food and exercise span a wide spectrum. Some of us work out because we enjoy it and it makes us feel good, some want to lose a few pounds and tone up, some hate the gym but are desperate to lose weight, others are addicted to it. Excessive exercising often goes hand in hand with eating disorders (I was hooked on running for years). The same goes for body image and self-esteem: some of us feel good about our bodies, some are quietly confident, others avoid looking in the mirror or undressing in front of their partners. Then there are those who actively hate their bodies, deny themselves food when hungry, or binge eat in secret. And we can vary wildly, depending on our mood, hormones, outfits, even the weather. I have days when I feel confident and attractive, and other days when I feel like an insignificant grey slug.

However extreme or mild our feelings, there is a near-universal acknowledgement these days that a slimmer body is a superior body, that our lives will be better when we shift the body fat. As I argued in *The Ministry of Thin*, losing weight has become the modern Holy Grail. And it's no longer just a feminine preoccupation: from the national newspapers to *Men's Health* magazine to Radio 4's *Woman's Hour*, to endless Tumblr and Instagram pages, we discuss weight loss and weight gain *ad nauseam*.

As the obsession with thin increases, the distinction between normal 'disordered' eating and actual eating disorders becomes blurred: mostly along the lines of intermittent fasting, calorie restriction or day-on, day-off regimes. Since 2012, the most popular diet has been 5:2, which prescribes normal eating for five days a week and severely reduced calories on the other two days.

We saw the introduction of an even more extreme version of the 5:2 diet in 2014 called 4:3 – where the semi-fasting days increase to three days a week, and the normal eating days decrease to four. Just to be clear, 5:2 and 4:3 are not wacky weight-loss plans: they're considered completely mainstream. Both regimes are publicised in national broadsheets, endorsed by well-respected journalists and followed by sensible, educated adults. Over a million Brits follow the 5:2 diet, semi-starving themselves several days a week.

Whether it's Atkins or 5:2 or whatever, these days it's normal to be on a diet. It is more difficult, and more daring, to say that you're happy with your body, than it is to hate it. As well as our negative inner monologue, and our self-critical shared dialogue, we're surrounded by linguistic reminders that we are at war with our own bodies. It's not only the images, showing us how perfect other women (i.e. models) are, and how imperfect we are; the language of advertising is carefully crafted too. If we aren't engaged in the 'battle of the bulge' we're being urged to 'conceal' and 'correct' flaws; to 'attack problem areas' and 'fight the flab'. The language of male bodies focuses on building strength, sculpting muscles and boosting endurance, whereas women are encouraged to reduce, to slim down, to diminish in size.

Remember Tracey Emin's words: '… the less of me there is the better'. Is it any wonder that she (and so many of us) feel this way when we are harangued from all sides with gym-guilt, reminded of the virtues of trimming down, toning up and getting rid of our 'excess' flesh?

Of course size matters: there are serious consequences to excessive consumption, inactivity and obesity, just as there are serious consequences to food restriction, over-exercising and emaciation. And yet we still can't have a rational debate about the health implications, because body weight is an issue fraught with fear and shame. In writing about anorexia I described the physical experience, because I believe it's important to understand – how your tailbone sticks out so you can barely sit on a wooden chair, how your limbs ache from lying in bed with no cushioning, how you bruise easily and feel cold pretty much constantly. How your ribs and your hips and your shoulder blades become this weird, coat-hanger arrangement of clashing bones. Anorexia makes women *and* men infertile: clobbering your ovaries and your sperm count. And just like obesity, anorexia can kill – it has the highest mortality rate of all mental illnesses.

If we desire above all else to be thin, we need to understand the triggers, traumas and possible long-term consequences. We need to look at the risks of these new extreme diets. No one knows whether an intermittent fasting diet can trigger an eating disorder, but it seems like a good place to start.

The desperate quest to get thin can turn into a colossal waste of time and money: the failed diets, the unused gym membership, the multiple daily thoughts of self-hatred.

Whether we exercise or not, it shouldn't make us dislike our own bodies. Children run and jump and play because they can; because it feels good. As adults we get stuck in negative cycles of guilt and self-recrimination, we're so weighed down with the sense of should and could: I *should* be working out, I *could* be slim if only I wasn't so lazy/greedy. It's the most pointless form of self-sabotage.

But are we going to spend our whole lives like this, feeling the wrong shape and the wrong weight in the wrong skin? You know the thought process: 'I'm single and lonely and no one will ever fancy me, so what's the point in trying to get fit?'; 'I've broken all the healthy rules already, so I might as well eat the rest of the pizza'. You hate yourself physically so you hate yourself mentally: failing becomes a self-fulfilling prophecy.

How can we break out of the negativity? The most important stage is to focus on health. Let go of the external pressures, ignore the magazines or images which make you feel inadequate. Remind yourself that you're more than just a number on the scales, a body shape or a clothes size. Nothing about you is flawed; nothing needs concealing or disguising (unless you choose to do so). No lasers or injections here please. If you struggle with self-esteem, challenge your inner voice, try to replace the negative thoughts with positive ones. Be bold: wear something outrageous, go the shops in your pyjamas or dance on your balcony in your underwear (I do this frequently). Think of the goals you're aiming for, the fun you can have, the people you can love, the change you can make in the world.

If it helps, while you're practising, visualise your body as a sleek machine – a healthy machine, which needs healthy fuel and healthy activity to keep it ticking over! The more you can override emotions like shame or self-hatred, the more you'll connect with what your body really needs. When you're listening to your body and trusting your hunger, the internal warfare slowly grinds to a halt.

It may sound odd, but I identified with the woman on the plane. I understand how extreme fatness acted as a form of protection; extreme thinness had worked the same way for me. Food is there when nothing else is, it's a reassurance, a crutch, and bingeing numbs you, just like starving. Not eating was my way of exerting control when my emotions felt overwhelming: becoming very thin or very fat, somehow becoming irrelevant, is a way of disappearing.

Fat or thin, insecure or confident, young or old, we all have body hang-ups. But in my experience, losing weight is not the route to happiness. Thinner does not equal happier. Love and family are infinitely more precious than the shrinking number on the scales. Remember the biblical advice: *treat others as you would want them to treat you*? Well how about this: *treat yourself as you would treat others*. A little kindness and respect, when we talk about our own bodies, could go a long way.

Of course it's not easy. It takes a thick skin and a strong will not to feel inadequate in our image-obsessed age. The negative inner voice won't fade easily: *Why are you so greedy? Why can't you stop eating? You're lazy and a loser; If you went to the gym you'd be slimmer, fitter, less flabby, more successful.* But really, the greatest success is being happy in one's own skin.

As always, the solution lies in taking back control over our thoughts and our body language. It's hard but not impossible. Just decide right now: no more self-criticism. You're not fat or ugly, you're interesting and unique. Our minds are more powerful than we realise and change is a choice. Either we can live in this state of perpetual discomfort, or we can change the way we think, talk and, gradually, the way we feel about our bodies.

I enjoyed this snippet from Cameron Diaz's *The Body Book*, in which she shows how to turn even the simplest activity (washing your face) into an act of love:

'Washing your face is self-nurturing... A moment to look in the mirror and say, "Good job today! You worked hard, you did your best." Or, "Tomorrow we can pick it up a little, I have confidence in you!"'

Talking to yourself in the mirror might feel strange, but at least it will make you smile!

Here are some final ideas for switching your attitude from negative to positive, and boosting your body confidence, which have helped me:

* **Be kind to number one:** Notice how you treat yourself: is it cruel or kind? No matter how worthless you feel, you deserve respect and nurture. Don't use food as a reward; don't use exercise as a punishment. Look after yourself as you would look after others. If you're struggling, ask yourself: what would I say to a good friend in this situation?

* **Keep things in perspective:** So you've broken your diet, skipped a spinning class or gained a few pounds – it's not the end of the world. Avoid catastrophising. Clear your head, step back from the situation and ask yourself if it will matter in a few months' time. Try to look at the bigger picture: you may feel your stomach is flabby, but what about your expressive eyes or captivating smile?

* **Positive Post-its:** Stick some upbeat mantras around your home – uplifting thoughts on the mirror or cheeky

compliments on the kettle. It sounds silly, but they can give you a boost! Who else is going to greet you with the words 'smile, you're amazing' every morning?

✳ **Find a new focus:** Look at busy, successful people – they don't have time for negativity. Our self-destructive feelings often stem from worrying too much about ourselves, so get busy! Pursue interests that are not related to food or exercise: get the focus off your own appearance. The more interesting you feel, the more attractive you will be to others.

✳ **Help others:** Volunteer at a care home for the elderly, get involved in a local community project, a library reading scheme or a gardening group. By helping others you'll also be helping yourself, making you feel good about yourself, inside and out.

✳ **Choose happiness:** You can't always control what happens to you, but you can control how you react. You can choose to see the bright side, associate with positive people and count your blessings. Seize opportunities and focus on daily pleasures. And when things go wrong, keep your cool. Build resilience, take the highs and the lows, learn from the bad times and appreciate the good.

✳ **Be here now:** Live in the present, for the present. Don't buy dresses or jeans that will fit you when you lose 10 lb – wear clothes you love, which fit you now. Donate anything that is too small or too big to a local charity shop and make the best of yourself today.

✳ **Step away from the scales:** Of course they have a place in the doctor's surgery, but you don't need to become a slave to your bathroom scales. If your morning weigh-in makes you feel like a failure all day, it's time to break the habit.

* **Redefine your terms:** Think in terms of nutritious eating and an active lifestyle, rather than 'losing weight'. If you do need to lose weight, find a happy, healthy reason for self-improvement. Most crash diets fail in the long-term because they're too punitive: make your positive changes last.

* **Stay SMART:** Set yourself Specific, Measurable, Attainable, Relevant, Time-bound goals. Focus on the health benefits for your body, rather than inches lost or the number on the scales. Choose activities you enjoy, so it's playful rather than painful, and exercise with friends for added motivation.

* **Change the script:** Ban negative body language from your vocabulary. Don't use the words 'fat' or 'ugly' about yourself or others, ever. This applies to celebrities and strangers as much as yourself and your friends. Don't refer to your flabby bits, bingo wings or muffin top. Don't scrutinise or criticise other women; look for the beauty in everyone. It takes time, but ending the verbal self-hatred is the only way to end the mental self-hatred.

* **If all else fails: simplify!** Remember that you only have one life. Treat each day like it's your last. Nothing much will matter in 100 years' time, so why not risk it? Why not risk being happy?

Chapter Three

TRULY, MADLY CONFIDENT

What would you do if you weren't afraid?

Throughout my 20s I asked myself this question, and every time the answer came back – write. I had never thought seriously of doing anything else; I knew one day I'd be a writer (when I was a grown-up) but the years went by and still I wasn't writing. Career-wise I was in the right ballpark, in that I was editing and publishing other people's books, but I wasn't putting my own pen to paper.

So what was holding me back? Lack of ideas? Lack of time? Lack of resources? Probably all of those things – but none of them amounted to a row of beans. If I didn't have ideas, I'd need to persevere: books do not spring fully formed from the page. If I didn't have time, I could get up a few hours earlier in the morning. As for resources, I had plenty of notebooks just waiting to be written in.

In truth, I had everything I needed but confidence. Starting anything new requires perseverance, patience and confidence. I had tried writing bits and bobs, first chapters of novels, outlines of articles, the odd poem, but they weren't very good. So instead of believing that I'd improve, instead of believing in myself, I gave up. But writing was my dream, so how could I keep giving up?

In the end it was another writer – a no-nonsense woman in her 90s – who galvanised me into action. I had cornered her at a drinks party and idiotically asked her: 'What's the secret to writing?' 'The secret?' she laughed derisively. 'There is no secret. To write, you have to write.' Over the next few months I started writing. I wrote through the bad stuff – there was a lot of it – and I just kept writing. I got up three hours before work and worked on my novel, and by the end of that first year, I had a finished manuscript, a weekly column in *The Times* and a literary agent. More than that, I began to believe in myself.

It wasn't as straightforward as it sounds. It took me another year to muster the confidence to resign from my secure job in publishing and start writing full-time. It took several more years (and a million rewrites) to get that first novel published. As well as the lack of financial security, being freelance was emotionally up and down at first. I had frequent existential crises, feeling directionless and out of the loop. I missed the camaraderie of colleagues and the gossip around the water cooler. But I gained an inner confidence, knowing that I was going after my dream. Instead of thinking about being an author and vaguely hoping it would happen someday, finally I was writing. I don't know why it was so hard, but it was. And it's one of the bravest things I've done.

What would *you* do if you weren't afraid? How would you answer this question – honestly?

Chances are, it's nothing to do with skydiving or trekking to the North Pole. I could jump out of a plane, but writing filled me with self-doubt. For many of us the thing we'd do if we weren't afraid is much closer to home: retraining for a new career, leaving an unhappy relationship, starting our own business, going on a date. Even relatively small-scale changes like these – though we may desperately want to make them – can fill us with fear. And what often stops us from changing our lives is not a lack of financial resources or physical courage, but a lack of confidence.

This question of what confidence looks like, and how women can get more of it, is highly topical these days. Books such as *Lean In* by Facebook's Sheryl Sandberg, a book that encourages women to grasp opportunities in the workplace, tap into a new mood of fearlessness. Gone are the days when female confidence meant power dressing, ball breaking and being 'one of the boys'. Replacing this is a quieter, subtler form of female fortitude, available to all of us because it comes from within. This is about healthy striving, not perfectionism or artifice. It's not about pretending to be something you're not, because nothing fuels insecurity like pretence. Rather it's facing one's fears and doubts, and being OK in the discomfort zone. Perhaps even pushing yourself *into* that discomfort zone. As the blogger and Twitter guru Mastin Kipp (@TheDailyLove) puts it: 'Fear is usually a compass pointing you in the direction that you should go.'

The funny thing about confidence is that it's mostly inside our heads. Confidence depends more on what we believe about ourselves than on the hard facts (e.g. qualifications, skills or experience), so minimising those negative beliefs is vital to boosting self-esteem. Repeatedly negative thought processes are known as 'limiting belief loops' and here's how they work:

Negative self-beliefs lead to inaction, which leads to no results, which confirm our insecurities, leading to more negative feelings and more negative thoughts. End result: demotivation.

Positive self-beliefs lead to positive action, which leads to encouraging results, which lead to positive feelings and more positive thoughts. End result: confidence.

In other words, our beliefs create our reality: a lack of self-confidence often leads to even greater insecurity.

As well as self-belief, it's important to set realistic goals. There is no point dreaming of becoming a supermodel if you're five foot nothing, or becoming a surgeon if you faint at the sight of blood. I have finally accepted that I'll never be a ballerina... I've kind of missed the boat! When we're striving for unattainable goals, fixating on our failings, or trying to be perfect, we will always fall short.

Why do we even try to be perfect? It's an impossible goal, and it's never-ending, and it stops us from being happy. Life itself is deeply imperfect, and there's a great liberation in accepting that. I remember, at the height of anorexia, how hard I found it to have people in my flat – whether family visits or birthday parties – because company is MESSY! How could I relax with friends when they might pull books off shelves, or spill their wine, or rearrange the cushions on the sofa? How could I enjoy my adorable baby nephew when he might jump on my immaculate bed, or smear banana on the walls? I needed everything to be perfect, but real life and real people are not.

My version of perfectionism – extreme self-discipline and control – was an extreme case of course. Taken to its logical conclusion, anorexia leads not to perfection but to death. However, the long and difficult process of recovery taught me a lot about letting go. Just as I had to accept that my writing, at first, would be bad; that I needed to practise, and find some courage and self-belief – so I needed self-belief to recover from anorexia. To make those life changes I had to accept my own imperfection.

Accepting one's own imperfection is remarkably liberating. Until we let go of perfect, that millstone around our neck, we cannot enjoy the present. It takes courage to say: my house/flat is chaos, but this party is wonderful. Or I feel happy and it doesn't matter that my hair is a mess. Or this man makes me laugh and I don't care that he's not conventionally handsome. Or I've failed my driving test for the fourth time, but I'll try again. Or I don't have the perfect body, but I'm strong enough to hike up mountains. It's the opposite of that needy, narcissistic whine: 'What does everyone think of me?' Instead it is saying: 'I am enough.' Best of all, it's realising something very simple: there are more interesting things out there than me.

Striving to be perfect is an emotional drain on others. What could be more tedious than someone who goes on and on about their faults? I remember when I was around 17 years old, one of my best friends, M, had severe acne. We were heavily into Indie music at the time, and went clubbing several evenings a week in the centre of London. Before going out, I'd plaster on black kohl eyeliner and mascara – aiming for the

Cleopatra look, but probably looking more like a goth. My friend M would use a very heavy foundation and concealer. God knows what we looked like; but we had this rule, that once we were out, no matter how crap we felt (her acne, my panda eyes) no moaning was allowed. We'd stand in front of the mirrors in the nightclub toilets – shocking lights – and repair our make-up as girls around us competed over who felt the most ugly, spotty or fat. M's skin condition was quite disfiguring, but she always smiled, and always got on with the evening. And she attracted plenty of male interest, because she was fabulous to be with.

We were only teenagers, but I learnt a lot from her positive attitude. How much more mature to accept that it's not all about you, or your minor flaws; how much more interesting to take your eyes off the mirror; how much more generous to focus on others. Until then, I'd believed that not being perfect was a sign of failure. Actually, accepting that you're imperfect is a sign of success.

The American author Anna Quindlen writes: 'The thing that is really hard, and really amazing, is giving up on being perfect and beginning the work of becoming yourself.' She's right: getting on with life, minus the drama, means being robust and resilient. In other words, being a grown-up.

It takes maturity to get outside ourselves, and it takes courage to appreciate what we have. Many self-help experts advocate keeping a daily gratitude journal for precisely this reason. It's a powerful skill, to enjoy what we're doing right now rather than regretting what we don't have, what we can't do, how we wish we were. It is harder than it sounds: to be thankful, positive and present.

Living in the present should come naturally to us, but in fact, being fully present is something children do better than adults. Observe a young child playing and marvel at their total absorption: they don't ask for Lego evaluation or feedback, feel insecure about their performance, or wonder what the current activity might be leading to. They are masters of a simple skill: focusing on the task at hand. As adults, we learn dissatisfaction, comparison, anxiety. We get tangled up in the past, we project ahead to the future and we lose the present moment, which is all we really have.

Getting properly absorbed is therapeutic. In recent years I've found deep absorption in activities such as skiing, and singing in a choir: these new skills are hard for me. Because I'm not a natural skier, it takes all my concentration and complete focus. I can't waste time worrying about how I'm skiing, because I'm focusing 100 per cent on not falling over. Similarly at choir practice, I don't have spare brainpower to worry about how I'm singing, because I'm focusing 100 per cent on trying to sight-read and hit the right notes. Being a 'beginner' as an adult, as I found when I started writing, demands self-belief.

In her 2012 book *Daring Greatly*, Dr Brené Brown writes about another enemy of the present moment, the concept of 'foreboding joy'. This describes a tendency we have to imagine the worst possible scenario in any situation: to anticipate disaster. Brown describes watching over her young children sleeping, moved to tears with the sense of joy, but almost unable to breathe, imagining terrible things happening to them. Although it's not logical, we've all done it – rehearsing future tragedy as a form of self-protection.

'Foreboding joy' explains why we often find it hard to enjoy what we have. Our most intense emotions make us vulnerable to heartbreak and grief, so we put up barriers. We're caught between the desperate need for certainty, and the awareness of how fragile and transitory human happiness can be. But we cannot spend our lives avoiding emotional exposure. If we open ourselves up at all, we risk losing.

Joy *does* make us feel vulnerable: it's rare and there is no guarantee that it will last. This explains why we find ourselves, in the midst of precious moments, terrified that something bad will happen next. It's an attempt to protect ourselves from future pain and disappointment, but all it does is mar the present.

Are you familiar with the 'Serenity Prayer'?

> *God, grant me the serenity to accept the things I cannot change, the courage to change the things I can, and the wisdom to know the difference.*

It has been adopted by Alcoholics Anonymous (and other twelve-step programmes) but we could all learn from it. The emphasis on acceptance of what one cannot change, alongside a willingness to remedy what one can, is powerful. Letting go of perfection does not mean living with really bad stuff, or giving up, or giving in. It's focusing on positive, realistic changes while making the best of what we have. It's about acknowledging our weak points and choosing instead to develop our strengths.

The behavioural therapist Deborah Fields has interesting ideas about self-acceptance: 'Why is it that we're able to soothe babies when they're born, yet we can't do it for ourselves? We have to learn to nurture ourselves, our battles, all the good and bad, so we can bounce back up.'

Letting go of perfection takes – and creates – confidence. It seems paradoxical, that being vulnerable should take strength, but it does. And vulnerability represents a deep and subtle form of power. A person who is able to be vulnerable is saying to the world: 'This is who I really am and I'm OK with that.'

I'm still discovering the power of vulnerability in my own life. I recently gave a talk at a girls' school on the subject of feminism, self-esteem and body image. Afterwards I was overwhelmed with questions from girls and women of all ages. As I was leaving, one of the teachers drew me aside. She'd struggled with binge eating for years, she said. This evening she had decided to go home and talk to her husband about it.

The next morning, a mother in her 40s emailed me, saying she'd been in the audience with her teenage daughter. Driving home, she had finally found a way to raise a difficult subject: 'I had severe anorexia for years and I've started to see signs in my daughter. We ended up sitting outside the house in the dark, talking in the car for ages. It was the best way to do it and we shared a lot of important stuff. I feel much happier now.'

The shame we have, the fear we feel, is in our own heads. As Brené Brown writes: 'Vulnerability sounds like truth and feels like courage.' The outside world doesn't judge you for being less than perfect. It doesn't condemn you for being truthful. When you lay open your own vulnerability, you empower yourself and others.

Rejecting perfectionism and being true to ourselves is not only vital for our personal confidence: it's also important in our careers. When we find work which absorbs us, and when we can find an authentic 'fit' between our daily nine-to-five activities and what we care about, we're more likely to feel that our lives have meaning. Having some alignment between our beliefs and values and how we spend our time makes a real difference to how satisfied we are with our lives, and how confident we feel. We're also more effective when we believe in what we do; when we're using our strengths, we're more likely to give our whole selves to the task at hand.

Of course we've all done jobs which have nothing to do with our personal interests – work pays the bills, and we can't always expect it to be deeply fulfilling. But I believe that whatever we do, we can do authentically. During my GCSEs and A levels, I had a weekend job in my local Woolworths: first as a cashier and then on the music counter. I devised various new systems for changing the Top 40 pop charts every Sunday and soon found myself enjoying what could have been a fairly repetitive process. I've taken a similar approach with countless bar, cafe and hotel jobs along the way: if we can't work at the peak of our creative powers, we can always build relationships with colleagues and customers, find fun in whatever we're doing. It's the essence of that phrase: 'If you can't do what you love, love what you do.'

As well as loving what we do, it's important to have clear boundaries between work, family and personal time. This requires confidence, particularly for women. Whereas traditional male roles as manager/employee/father/breadwinner have stayed relatively consistent for decades, female roles have changed radically. The changes are positive and negative: women argued for more independence, more pay, more seniority, more respect, but in getting this, many are now effectively doing two full-time jobs. We have gained greater power in the workplace while still doing the majority of cooking, cleaning and child-rearing. According to the campaigning group UK Feminista, women undertake far more childcare and housework than men. They estimate that women who work, with or without children, spend 15 hours a week on average doing chores, while men spend only five.

Of course, men are increasingly involved in family life (with some even staying at home as so-called house husbands) but they are in the minority: domesticity remains an overwhelmingly female domain. In the UK, at least 75 per cent of mothers have primary responsibility for childcare in the home.

This is why women need confidence: to challenge the ingrained cultural notions of men as providers and women as carers. We need confidence to pursue those promotions and stand up to sexism and fight for equal pay, without getting pissed off at all the contradictions. We need confidence to survive and thrive in male-oriented workplaces.

Despite these ongoing gender inequalities in the workplace, and in the media, the situation is not entirely hopeless. Slowly things *are* changing. Women of all ages are starting to challenge the stereotypes, and to forge their own identities beyond the tired old formulae of wife and stay-at-home mother, or power-hungry career woman. After decades of striving for the perfect body, family or career, and feeling guilty when we fail, there is a new mood of optimism. There is a new honesty, a desire for a real work–life balance, and a re-definition of success beyond money and power. Many women are finding the confidence to go back to university or retrain, to launch their own business, to step up or 'lean in'. We can't always defeat those gender inequalities, but we can decide to overcome the fear that has consistently held us back.

Fear is a strong word, but it's one of the main barriers women face, personally and professionally. I've often felt that fear: of not being liked, of appearing pushy or over-ambitious, of not doing things right, of making bad decisions, of being a failure or a laughing stock, of not following the path other women have followed. Just the other day, at dinner with my boyfriend and his mother, I found myself wondering if I was being too talkative, if she'd prefer her son to be with someone quieter, less opinionated. What a ridiculous thing to worry about.

Fear also leads to imposter syndrome, that sense of being a fraud and that our incompetence is about to be found out. I have female friends who are undeniably successful – in banking, advertising, publishing – who still express private insecurities about their capabilities. While anyone can experience imposter syndrome, women tend to suffer worse than men. Despite being experts in their field, they routinely underestimate their own skills and underplay their own achievements.

US comedian Tina Fey is amusing on this. In an interview with the *Independent* in 2010, she said: 'The beauty of the imposter syndrome is you vacillate between extreme egomania, and a complete feeling of: "I'm a fraud! Oh God, they're on to me!..." Seriously, I've just realised that almost everyone is a fraud, so I try not to feel too bad about it.'

Perhaps it's unsurprising that we downplay our own achievements, when you consider the cultural suspicion – even disapproval – of female success. From childhood, little girls are expected to be modest, self-effacing and not to brag. There is an implicit cost in being too capable. Just look at the derogatory words we use for women who are capable: pushy, ambitious, strident, aggressive, bossy. Men, on the other hand, are described as commanding, authoritative, born leaders. Forceful or competitive women are viewed with suspicion, as if they were unnaturally masculine, somehow unladylike. Perhaps it's no wonder that we experience self-doubt.

Self-doubt can also be a form of self-defence: downplaying our achievements becomes a way of protecting ourselves. Remember the saying: 'Pride comes before a fall'? It's easier to put ourselves down before others can.

Whether or not we actively put ourselves down, we all know how hard it can be simply to accept a compliment graciously, without excuses or embarrassment. How many times have you heard yourself saying things like: 'It wasn't really my work, it was a team effort.' (It can be even harder to accept personal compliments: 'This old thing? Oh it's just something I dragged out of the laundry – and God my roots need doing.')

Because of the implicit disapproval around female success, it's essential to cultivate resilience. The fact is, when you speak your mind, or reach the top, you inevitably offend someone. I remember my first female boss telling me: 'You can't be a successful woman without making enemies.' It hurts to be criticised or disliked, especially for those of us who care too much about what others think. However, being resilient doesn't mean being entirely without emotions. Simply that we feel the emotion – sadness, anger, whatever – and then move on.

Confidence comes from living authentically, at home and at work. Increasingly, it doesn't feel like failure to admit that you have emotions, that your family matters as much as your career, that you want meaningful work *and* good personal relationships, just like other women.

Still, work and child-rearing can be an uphill struggle for women. Any mother who has ever sat in an afternoon meeting glancing anxiously at the clock (while men massage each other's egos) or slunk out of the office at 4 p.m. to collect her children, knows this. My friend Jo (who works in banking) says: 'You feel guilty, despite knowing you're putting in the hours, often far more effectively than others... when you have to leave early to do pick-up, or work from home while looking after a sick child, you just feel like a skiver.'

The guilt and anxiety is only part of it. The 'motherhood penalty' is a term coined by sociologists who argue that working mothers encounter systematic disadvantages in pay, perceived competence and benefits, relative to childless women. The penalty may even result in a pay gap between non-mothers and mothers that is larger than the gap between men and women. Working mothers may also be perceived as less committed to their jobs, less dependable and less authoritative than non-mothers.

Despite the fact that procreation is quite an important function in the grand scheme of things, the motherhood penalty is alive and well in many offices. *The New York Times* recently wrote about 'the motherhood penalty vs the fatherhood bonus'. It explained that while having children is bad for a woman's promotion and pay prospects, for men, having children is good for their careers. While mothers are less likely to be hired, perceived as competent or paid as much as their male counterparts, fathers are more likely to be hired than childless men and paid better after they have children.

According to UK Feminista, up to 30,000 women are sacked each year simply for being pregnant and each year an estimated 440,000 women lose out on pay or promotion as a result of pregnancy.

Childless/childfree women face hurdles too, simply by virtue of their gender. Anyone who has ever gone for a job interview in her late 20s or early 30s has been aware of the unspoken question: *Will she leave and have babies?* Employers may claim they don't take this into account when deciding between male and female applicants, but they do. Although the Sex Discrimination Act was passed in 1975 to protect female employment rights and opportunities, women still suffer prejudicial treatment from prospective employers. Employers such as Alan Sugar, for example; speaking about maternity rights and legislation in an interview with the *Daily Telegraph* in 2008, the self-made millionaire made these delightful comments: 'Everything has gone too far. We have maternity laws where people are entitled to too much. If someone comes into an interview and you think to yourself *there is a possibility that this woman might have a child and therefore take time off* it is a bit of a psychological negative thought. If they are applying for a position which is very important, then I should imagine that some employers might think *this is a bit risky...* By law I am not allowed to say to her, "Hold on love, do you think you are going to be able to cope in this job, you have to get the kids sorted?" That's the bottom line, you're not allowed to ask so it's easy – just don't employ them.'

Government figures from 2014 show that, despite the introduction of additional paternity leave in 2011, fewer than one in 50 new fathers are using their right to extra time off if their partner goes back to work. Until men contribute more to the domestic sphere, women will struggle to balance work and family life. Whatever our personal situation, we have a lot to juggle and it's easy to feel that we're failing – that we should look youthful, flawless and slim, while also being the perfect mother, daughter, wife, girlfriend, manager or superwoman.

But there is a groundswell of female self-assurance: more honesty and less nonsense about 'having it all' than in the past. These days there is more realism over what we really want from our careers, relationships and family. And there is no doubt we have more choices (even if we often feel judged for them). A decade ago, just one in nine women remained child-free at 45; in 2014 that figure is close to one in four.

The situation for women may still be far from ideal, but we're gaining the confidence to question the social norms and chart our own course. We may not always get it right, or be totally sure of the choices we've made, but genuine confidence isn't about being 'perfect'. It grows from self-knowledge and self-belief, and an ability to cope with life's ups and downs. We can't control what happens – things go wrong for all of us at times – but confident women have the resilience to keep going.

Confidence gives us a backbone, but it also gives us flexibility. Think of a confrontation you've faced, at home, college, in the office, in a public place. Which strategy works better: to fly off the handle and walk out in a fit of rage, or to state your case calmly and clearly, listen to the other side and reach a resolution? I spent years doing the former; now I aim for the latter. Like a tree in the wind, it's far stronger to be flexible and bend, than to be rigid and snap.

Showing our flaws is not only honest, it's also what draws us to others. The psychologist Dr Robert Glover argues that imperfection is a virtue: 'Humans are attracted to each other's rough edges.'

At a recent conference I talked about 'coming out'; standing up in your life and speaking your truth, whatever that truth might be: 'I'm lonely' or 'I'm an alcoholic' or 'I'm gay'. Saying the thing you're most ashamed of and dealing with it. Many people in the audience nodded when I said this. There is something liberating about not hiding: what could be more successful than being who you really are?

A whole woman – or man – is brave enough to put themselves out there. Vulnerability is part of authenticity and authenticity is the key to personal confidence. As my great-aunt Virginia Woolf wrote: 'If you do not tell the truth about yourself you cannot tell it about other people.'

Chapter Four

BUILDING TRUE CONFIDENCE

I remember years ago, when I was on my way to (what felt like) the most important interview of my life. I was 21, recently graduated and in the final round for a job I desperately wanted with an advertising agency. It was an icy morning and I slipped on my way up the stone steps of their imposing Soho headquarters. I fell hard, ripped my black opaque tights quite spectacularly, and gashed open my shin. I had no spare tights, and no time to do anything except rush into the ladies bathroom, dab my bleeding leg with wet tissues and take a few deep breaths. Then I took my tights off and turned them around, so the huge ladder went up the back, not the front.

I got the job. A few months later I asked my boss what they'd made of my unusual appearance that day, tights on the wrong way round and ripped up the back. 'Ripped?' he said. 'I thought your presentation was great. I didn't notice the tights.'

When I fell on the steps, I had a choice, although it didn't feel like it at the time. I could burst into tears and give up, find a shop to buy more tights and risk arriving late – or I could just clean myself up, put my tights on back to front and get on with it. I was acting confident, even though I was shaken – but I was also being authentic. To me, the two go hand in hand: authenticity is a key aspect of confidence.

Of course, with authenticity comes vulnerability, and this is the other key aspect of confidence: bringing your whole self – including your fears and vulnerabilities – to whatever you do. Confidence doesn't mean you'll never get nervous, before an interview, say, or speaking in public. In fact, jittery nerves provide the adrenalin rush that gets you ready to perform, excel. But when you're being *real* – when you know your subject and feel passionate about it – these jitters are positive. When you're being genuine, you can't be found out. That's why authenticity is a winner.

I believe we can all become more confident. Not through assertiveness training, not through bluffing or bulldozing others – simply by drawing on our inner resources. Here are some of the strategies I use, when I'm floundering, to remind me where my strengths lie.

FIND YOUR FLOW

Nothing builds confidence like being good at what you do – and loving it. 'Flow', a term coined in 1975 by the psychologist Mihaly Csikszentmihalyi, is a state of complete absorption when we're totally concentrated on what we're doing; when our emotions are positive, energised and aligned with the task at hand. The idea of flow is identical to the feeling of being 'in the zone' or 'in the groove'. Whether it's writing or dancing, sailing or jewellery making, we've all had the experience of being in the moment, so immersed that hours fly by. We forget about the clock, or lunch, or our own worries, and nothing else seems to matter.

It's rare that this 'flow' activity is what we do for a living, but there are ways to integrate our talents into our work, especially within the digital marketplace. My friend Ilya is a lawyer, but in her spare time she makes exquisite silk dresses, the Japanese art of shibori (a highly skilled form of tie-dye). On the Internet, she has met artists and designers who have helped her develop her technique. What started as a private passion may even become a fully fledged business: she recently sold her first dress on eBay.

From evening classes to online courses to social meet-up groups, there are plenty of ways to nurture your unique talents. We tend to enjoy what we're good at, so developing your skills makes you happier and more competent. Improving yourself also promotes natural self-esteem, and when you respect your own abilities, there's less time to worry about so-called flaws.

True confidence is also about accepting what you're not great at. Maybe you're a hopeless public speaker but you're great one-on-one; or you'll never be supermodel slim but you're an amazing cook. We can't have it all and it makes more sense to be realistic, and value our individual talents. Building our lives around what we love is a good foundation for happiness and confidence.

TRUST YOUR GUT

The brain and the gut are intimately linked, so it's worth listening to that 'gut feeling'. From danger radar to stress detectors, our humble guts are powerful, sometimes life-saving, messengers. Forget weighing up the options, many experts believe we'd do well to listen to our bodies. *Blink: The Power of Thinking Without Thinking*, by Malcolm Gladwell, has been on the bestseller lists since 2005 (and is reportedly on the Prime Minister's bedside table too). In it Gladwell argues that good decision-making is about learning to trust your instincts – literally, the feeling in your gut. In the Internet age, it's easy to have too much information – resulting in what Gladwell calls 'analysis paralysis'. Instead he advocates simplifying the decision-making process: 'If the big picture is clear enough, then decide from the big picture without using a magnifying glass.' Learning to listen to – and trust – our gut takes practice, but over time it can become a valuable and reliable guide.

We can develop our gut instinct in a couple of simple ways:

Decision-making

We assume we should make decisions with our brains, but actually our bodies are powerful decision-makers too. Choose a situation in which you're wavering between two options. First think about one side – for example, 'I want to resign and find a new job.' While you're thinking this, notice the sensation in your gut. Do you feel a tightening, a gripping? Softening, spaciousness, warmth? Do you feel comfortable or uneasy? Now shift to the other side of the issue – 'I want to stay in my current job.' Again, tune in to how your gut feels and what kind of thoughts arise. You may not get a definite answer at first, but the more you listen to your body, the more you'll develop a clear gut sense. It's not about right and wrong; it's about which decision *feels* right.

Danger radar

Gut feelings also help you work out whether a person or situation is good or bad for you. Think back to a time when someone or something made you feel upset or unsettled (even if you're not sure why). Recall that difficult experience and notice what happens in your body. Do you feel tense or relaxed, comfortable or uncomfortable? Is there a knot in your stomach, a lump in your throat? Practise being aware of how your body reacts physically to thoughts and situations. Although you don't always have to act on them, these are important signals.

The gut is also an excellent barometer of stress. Next time you feel anxious or uneasy, try a simple visualisation exercise. Find a memory or place that is special to you, maybe walking beside the sea or playing your favourite song. Whatever comes to mind, focus on the details that make this meaningful: the sounds, colours, textures or smells. As you visualise this 'happy' time or place, you'll feel your gut becoming softer and your body more relaxed.

PLOUGH YOUR OWN FURROW

Do it *your* way! It can be stressful, especially for women, trying to meet the expectations of society, our families and ourselves. You can do wonders for your confidence by deciding, here and now, to ignore the 'life blueprint'. Stop comparing yourself to others: who cares if you're not married by 30, or if you're still renting at 40? So what if you decide you're not cut out for motherhood, or you prefer the company of your dogs to a man?

The most liberating decision you can make is to follow your own heart and be authentic. It may sound selfish, but it's not: you'll be happier when you stop panicking about what you haven't achieved. When you stop comparing yourself with others, the sky's the limit. Look at the success of Lady Gaga, a pop singer who favours PVC leotards, outlandish hair topiary and dresses made of raw meat. Perhaps it's no wonder that as 'perfect' female beauty becomes increasingly homogeneous, Gaga's zaniness is appealing. She has over 42 million followers on Twitter (just behind Barack Obama) and near-cult-like status among her acolytes, whom she calls her 'Little Monsters'. She tweets about this: 'Being different is a talent. You illuminate what makes you special in the sea of sameness around you.'

Individualism is something to be proud of, and there's nothing more confidence boosting than going your own sweet way. Personally, I adore actresses like Julia Roberts and Meryl Streep, who are beautiful in an unconventional way, and whose personality shines through. I love *Sex and the City* star Sarah Jessica Parker for her quirky, sometimes bonkers, style.

FEEL THE FEAR

Bravery is a crucial part of confidence. There's a reason why *Feel the Fear and Do It Anyway* is still the bestselling self-help book of all time, more than 25 years after it first appeared, and why many readers (myself included) credit this book with changing their lives. Author Susan Jeffers identified that 'what if' feeling which holds us back and encourages us to face those fears. The single most powerful piece of advice in the book? 'Whatever happens, I'll be OK'.

Of course we can't eliminate fear, nor should we. Like gut instinct, fear is a useful barometer in dangerous situations. But we shouldn't allow fear to stop us from taking risks, or making changes – instead we need to use it to get where we want to be. This doesn't mean that we'll never feel wobbly or nervous; everyone puts on a brave face at times. Learning to appear confident when your knees feel like jelly is a really important life skill. As is picking yourself up and carrying on when you've messed up (or ripped your tights to shreds). When you fail, fail forward.

Here's a strategy I use to get a handle on fear and indecision: divide a piece of paper into two columns and write down the FEAR at the top of the page. It could be trivial or serious: losing your job or your home, leaving your partner, turning 30 or 50, losing a parent or getting cancer. In the left-hand column describe that fear in detail, then write down in the right-hand column how you might deal with it. Think deeply about what you're scared of – and then work out what is the absolute worst that can happen? The truth is, we almost always cope. The fear is usually greater than the reality.

BAN BITCHINESS

And stop sniping. Building confidence in others is a wonderful way to forge bonds and boost your own confidence. We're all guilty of the occasional flash of *schadenfreude*, but it's illogical: calling someone else ugly or stupid doesn't make you prettier or cleverer. We don't need to undermine other women in order to excel.

One of the joys of my life in recent years has been rediscovering how fantastic women can be. During our teens and 20s we fall in and out of love/lust, or we get distracted planning the best ever wedding, or we're constantly busy with children or career building. It's easy to assume our friends will always be around, and we all know women who drop their friends as soon as they get a new man. Actually we need to invest time and care in our friendships, just as we do in our romantic relationships. At my rock-bottom moments, my closest female friends, my sisters and my mother have been there.

It took me years to realise how precious female friendship can be. I was moved to discover a similar sentiment expressed by Virginia Woolf, a century ago: 'The truth is, I often like women. I like their unconventionality. I like their completeness. I like their anonymity.'

A fundamental difference with the new form of female confidence is that it's not back-stabbing or bitchy. Authenticity means having the confidence to support others, especially in the workplace. The best female bosses always look out for their staff and give credit where it's due. As former US Secretary of State Madeleine Albright observed: 'There is a special place in hell for women who don't help other women.'

Daily Mail journalist Samantha Brick agrees that we should extend kindness to others, especially when they're being nasty. She was publicly vilified for **that** *Daily Mail* article in 2012 ('Women hate me because I'm beautiful') and received around 5,000 abusive messages via the comments section of the website. She continues to write articles about her high self-esteem and her irresistibility to the opposite sex – and of course she continues to receive angry responses. However, she refuses to let it dent her inner confidence: 'As someone in the public eye, whenever I find myself the subject of a personal critical attack, I honestly never take it to heart. One of my mantras is never to judge people – we're all doing the best we possibly can, and I don't pay any attention to those who judge me without knowing me. Granted I'm far from perfect, but I know myself well enough to know what my faults are. Instead I'm more likely to wonder... what have I said that's touched a nerve in their lives or caused them to lash out?'

Brick's words are a reminder that we don't need to attack other women. Female solidarity empowers ourselves and others.

STOP SAYING SORRY!

The new confidence is not bitchy or competitive, but nor is it apologetic. Saying sorry is something women excel at: we minimise our own achievements and give the credit to others, we defer well-meant compliments with self-deprecation. No more putting ourselves down when someone tells us they love our dress. Let's try saying 'thank you' – and nothing else! When we value ourselves from the inside, we're able to accept praise without apology.

FINALLY, LEARN TO TAKE CRITICISM

True confidence gives us the strength to accept constructive feedback without falling apart, or running to the bathroom in tears. To me, this is really important. It doesn't mean we don't feel hurt or upset – we are not bulletproof – but that we can bounce back. Nothing is more pointless than taking spiteful comments about you to heart, except allowing them to destroy you! But some criticism is valid and helpful.

If we can listen to criticism we become resilient; we learn how to take risks and make mistakes. Because there's nothing wrong with messing up: every successful leader knows that failure is part of success. As Richard Branson says: 'You don't learn to walk by following rules. You learn by doing, and by falling over, and it's because you fall over that you learn to save yourself from falling over.'

Of course it can be hard when you're in the eye of the storm, a crisis at work, or a row with your best friend, but don't let mistakes destroy your self-belief. Hillary Clinton has some refreshing advice: 'Take criticism seriously, but not personally. If there is truth or merit in the criticism, try to learn from it. Otherwise, let it roll right off you.'

The great thing about confidence is that it's truly self-defining: no one else can say what confidence means for you. You don't need to be loud, bubbly or wildly sociable, because confidence is available to introverts and extroverts alike. It's not about quantifiable achievements or millions in the bank, it's about authenticity.

Authenticity isn't without its risks: at times, being true to yourself will come at a cost. Not everyone reacts well to honesty, and not everyone will like you when you stand up, or stand out, for what you believe in. Authenticity won't necessarily make your life smooth, but in the end it will win you respect from one of the most important people in it: yourself.

Remember that old saying, 'What doesn't kill you makes you stronger'? Well, it also makes you more confident. The more you fail, the more you learn and grow, and the stronger you become. Paradoxically, the failures, disasters and naysayers in our lives are our biggest ally, because when things fall apart and you're still standing – that's the greatest confidence trick of all.

Chapter Five

ADVENTURES IN FOOD

There is a glorious moment in the film version of *Eat, Pray, Love*, Elizabeth Gilbert's bestselling memoir. Julia Roberts, playing the author Liz, and her Swedish friend Sofi, are in Naples to seek out what they have been told is the best pizzeria in Italy. The place is tiny, packed with locals and the food looks delicious.

They're tucking into large slices of margherita pizza with gusto, when Liz announces: 'I'm in love. I'm having a relationship with my pizza.' Her friend Sofi suddenly stops eating and starts to look anxious. She confesses that she hasn't stopped eating since she arrived in Italy. In a low voice, she says she must have gained at least 10 lb. Liz replies: 'In all the years you've ever undressed in front of a gentleman, has he ever asked you to leave? Has he ever walked out? Why not? Because he doesn't care. He's in a room with a naked girl...' You can hear the women of the world cheering. She's right: where we see cellulite or flab or a few extra pounds, our partners see gorgeous naked female flesh.

Liz says she has spent too many years denying herself the pleasures of food. She's sick of depriving herself, sick of working out how many calories she has eaten each day. Most of all, she's sick of feeling guilty.

Many of us know this guilt. I spent far too many years governed by the self-loathing she describes. The mere mention of food made me anxious and if I allowed myself to eat anything indulgent I was filled with guilt. In the end it was easier to avoid food altogether, to dodge all social eating situations with friends or family and never to eat unknown or unsafe ingredients.

Now that I'm recovered, I wonder why I wasted all that time and energy. What exactly was I avoiding? Did I think my loved ones were going to poison me? That they had a secret agenda to *make me fat*?

It took a long time, but the more I practised ignoring the anorexic voice, the quieter it became. These days I remember why eating out is a treat. It's a social activity, a way to unwind at the end of a long week, and an adventure: poring over the menu, quizzing the waiter about the specials, discussing the wine list. Swapping forkfuls with friends, experimenting with new flavours, tasting each other's dishes. I used to see food as a threat; now I realise it can be a pleasure.

Not being able to eat is more than a mental illness or a physical problem. It's a huge social handicap. From work lunches to family weddings to romantic evenings, not eating with others keeps you isolated and lonely. It prevents spontaneity. Eating together is a celebration; a way to bond with others; in the right company, it can be sexy, intimate. But what if eating fills you with fear?

My food fears held me back throughout my 20s. I recall starting new jobs, chatting with colleagues and getting on well until the inevitable question: 'We're taking our sandwiches to the park, are you coming?' Or 'join us at the pub for Friday fish and chips?', let alone the frequent business lunches. Avoiding food meant finding excuses, avoiding others, eventually appearing stand-offish: not a good way to forge friendships. I couldn't blame my colleagues in the end for not including me – would you persevere with someone who always turned you down? And yet I felt left out when I saw them leaving in a happy, hungry group at lunchtime.

It was even worse with new relationships and being invited out for dinner. It's completely normal to suggest food – even if it's just a few bar snacks – on an evening out. There is only so much alcohol you can consume on an empty stomach, and it creates tension if you refuse to eat. Men are generally unrestrained in their love of food, and most men – contrary to what we are led to believe as little girls (that we should have dainty, restrained, 'ladylike' appetites) – enjoy sharing this activity with women. They might like us to look slim, but most would far rather share a proper meal with us than watch us picking at a salad.

We look indulgently on our brothers, boyfriends and sons with their hearty appetites, while knowing we shouldn't eat with the same relish (in public) lest we appear greedy. For me it was even more confusing, because I hated eating in front of *anyone*, male or female; I wasn't sure if women were meant to have healthy appetites or be constantly watching their weight. Those extreme diets I read about in magazines: was that what other women really ate?

I lost all sense of what was normal. The thinner I became, the more of an ordeal eating out became. Was it OK to order a couple of starters, or just a salad? Could I ask for the dressing on the side? What if there was *nothing* safe on the menu? When friends said they were 'looking forward' to amazing meals with their boyfriends, I didn't get it at all. Being taken to a restaurant for my birthday sounded like the worst present in the world.

Anorexia made relationships exceptionally difficult. Just recently I found some emails from my dad, sent around five years ago.

Em, a word before your special dinner-date this evening. I know it may seem obvious, but often the obvious is overlooked. At the risk of sounding tiresome, I want to remind you that whether you're male or female, food on a date is important. I realise this is a problem – perhaps even THE problem – but going out with someone who isn't eating is, well, no fun. I've done it; found myself tucking into a delicious steak and kidney pie opposite a lady friend who is picking at a lettuce leaf. As your great-uncle Leonard said: "Everything is important and nothing is important." I think he would have agreed that on a date with someone you really like, dinner is important. Try to relax, soldier. D xx

And later, when I was STILL panicking over the menu and looking up the restaurant website and ringing my mum and generally making a mountain out of a mouthful...

Em, this could be the real breakthrough, when you rediscover that food can be one of life's real pleasures. You don't have to start off with double helpings – choose something modest and you can do it. This may be obvious, but you'll gradually realise that meals are not just refuelling but one of the things that really bring people together. Relax and give it a go, even if it means pretending. Hopefully the nosh will be irresistible and you'll find yourself thinking 'hey, this is good'. Remember you're back in the real world now, where people eat meals. Like I told you, no one wants to be with a girl however bright and attractive who doesn't eat. Tell yourself, this is a small thing which you have to start and may hold the key to changing your life. Take it as it comes. It may be wonderful. Do I sermonise? Sorry – I just want things to go right. Best of luck, and lots of love, D xx

These emails made me smile – I don't even recall which boyfriend I was seeing, or which date I was panicking about! They also capture all the unnecessary drama I built up around food.

What a difference a few years make. Recently my boyfriend and I went out for dinner at Cicada, a Pan-Asian restaurant in Clerkenwell, in central London. It was a Friday evening and I was wearing my new Pearl Lowe dress with black suede ankle boots and bare legs. We ordered Very Berry Martinis and watched the media crowd in the bar and outside on the street, sipping cocktails, wine and beers, flirting, chatting and smoking while they waited for their tables. The restaurant was a combination of Asian-inspired cuisine – 'fusion' food, but without the pretentiousness that usually implies. The decor was simple but stylish, with curved banquettes, mirrored walls and parquet flooring, and the atmosphere was chilled out and friendly. The dining booths were lit by tiny candles and there was mellow sitar music playing in the background.

For starters we shared mixed sashimi and dim sum. My main course was vegetable pad Thai: a platter of Singapore noodles, spicy cashew nuts, veggie tempura and fragrant steamed rice. Most of these were formerly 'forbidden' foods (noodles! nuts!) but I enjoyed every mouthful. It was a large portion, but I didn't freak out because – guess what – I know now that I don't have to finish it all. And so what if I consume something that is high in calories or fat? No one ever got obese from eating the occasional indulgent meal; it's not physically possible. And anyway, I need to let go – delicious dinners are part of the plan.

I even ordered dessert (unheard-of behaviour): a pomegranate and passion fruit sorbet, refreshing with our espressos. It was a clear, dark evening and we meandered home under the stars. There's an iPhone app which you hold up to the night sky and it shows you all the planets, galaxies, constellations and satellites. My boyfriend held up his phone and pointed out the North Star and Orion. It's amazing what's out there. Food, stars… I still had so much to discover.

There are turning points in any journey, although often we don't register them at the time. I remember one such point four years ago, visiting my brother Philip in Frankfurt, where he lives with his wife and two little boys. After a lovely weekend of sightseeing, shopping and catching up, we ended up at one of the Christmas markets.

German Christmas markets are legendary. As well as being packed with stalls selling gifts and toys, wood carvings, marionettes, candles, leather bags and jewellery, the market was overflowing with food. Bratwurst sausages, fried potatoes, *sauerkraut*, red cabbage, roast pork and suckling pigs on spits, all smelling heavenly. The desserts were just as enticing: toffee apples, Berliners – German doughnuts filled with jam and custard, topped with marshmallows and strawberries. There was Black Forest gateau and traditional gingerbread biscuits coated in chocolate, there was candied orange peel, raisins and almonds and cardamom. Mulled red wine was heated and spiced with cinnamon sticks, vanilla pods, cloves, citrus and sugar, served with rum, amaretto and cream. There were crepes topped with Nutella, marzipan and Grand Marnier. There was cider and *kirschwein,* made with ripe morello cherries.

Despite being a vegetarian, I can tell you that *all* the food at that Christmas market was mouth-watering. Or should I say the smell of the food, because of course I couldn't join in. My brother and his wife demolished herby smoked sausages in huge soft buns, and large steins of wheat beer; the children tucked into plates of *käsespätzle*, which are noodles topped with cheese, and *kartoffelknödel,* potato dumplings. They rounded off with slabs of stollen and mugs of mulled wine, and *heiße schokolade* for the kids.

I found a fruit stall and bought something 'safe' to eat. Walking back through the falling snow to join the others, listening to the Christmas carols, I felt sad. Sad and cold and tired of avoiding food – and so hungry. New experiences and tastes, smoked sausages and gingerbread biscuits, this is what travelling, holidays and family are all about. What was I doing in that German Christmas market eating a bloody apple?

I go through obsessional phases with food. I had a spell of eating a lot of hummus, then switched to tzatziki and pitta bread, then superfood couscous from M&S. I got addicted to mozzarella and tomato salad, then I became obsessed with the M&S pasta, pesto and pine nuts salad, drenched in olive oil. At the moment I'm eating a lot of wild rice, roasted vegetables and feta cheese, inspired by a recent holiday in the Camargue. Oh and Greek yogurt, eaten with juicy blueberries.

Obviously, one of the most important aspects of this journey has been letting go of control over food. For years I had been controlling every single thing that went into my body – it had to be pure and it had to be healthy. If possible it also had to be fresh and cold. Looking back, I can see that the control was even more of a problem than actual calorie restriction: I was eating enough to stay alive, but I wasn't eating in a way that allowed me to live fully, among others, in a happy way.

So how did I gain weight? The first thing to say is that it took years, and that it emphatically wasn't a linear process. More like three steps forward, then two steps back. Throughout my 20s I hovered between six and seven stone; as soon as I got near a healthy BMI I'd cut back, terrified, and lose weight again. It took years of practice: I was psyching myself up, I suppose; or testing the water. Maybe I got bored of anorexia. Or maybe I was just tired.

It's unbelievably tiring, having such a life-inhibiting neurosis. If that sounds melodramatic, it's not: anorexia affects every area of your life. I existed in a state of heightened anxiety, on the lookout for potential (food) threats during every waking moment. Imagine living in constant fight-or-flight mode: defensive and over-alert and starving hungry.

It's a shock, even now, to realise how stressful anorexia was. In spring 2014 I was speaking at a conference on emotional eating. One of the other speakers was the therapist Deborah Fields. Curvy, attractive and clever, with hair dyed bright pink and purple, I warmed to her immediately. 'I turn 50 next year,' she said, in her opening remarks, 'and you know what? I feel happy, confident and sexy. I honestly love who I am.' Isn't that revolutionary from a woman these days?

Deborah took out a large bag of small bouncy balls and distributed them among the audience. She asked us to hold them out, at arm's length, while she was speaking. After five minutes the lactic acid began to build up in our muscles, and soon everyone was putting their arms down to rest. 'That's what it's like,' Deborah said, 'living with a problem like overeating or undereating. It's not that the ball is heavy, or holding it that's hard – it's *keeping on* holding it that is hard; the sheer weight of carrying this burden around with you ALL OF THE TIME… It takes its toll.'

It would be inaccurate to say that I recovered because I got tired of carrying that burden around. In fact, recovery was extremely hard. Every 'extra' calorie I ate made me feel greedy, fat, out of control. I slowly increased the amount I was eating, very gradually, so that I could stay within my safe boundaries. In practice, this meant I was living primarily on fruit and vegetables, with the occasional wholemeal roll for variety.

Didn't I get bored of eating the same plain stuff day in, day out? What about all those ingredients I was missing out on: didn't I crave exciting spices, rich flavours, creamy sauces? Actually, no. When you're not eating much, every mouthful is precious. Unknown food was far too risky, because who knows what it might contain? If I had been forced to eat everything, I wouldn't have eaten anything.

If a meal in public was unavoidable – dinner out, a business lunch – I'd have soup or salad. If all else failed, I'd order pasta with a simple tomato sauce, and eat half. I knew of course that it would have been better to eat the whole plate of pasta, but half was better than nothing. Maybe my recovery needed to find its own pace.

Gradually, I started to gain weight. The panic receded. I began to rejoin the real world. My big fear, that giving up anorexia would leave a gaping hole in my life, did not come to pass. The gaping hole was a figment of my imagination. The less time I gave to anorexic thoughts, the more the rest of the world rushed in to fill that gap.

Most people don't have eating disorders, but there are plenty of disordered eating habits around – and is it any wonder we have become so confused about food? Alongside the health warnings, scaremongering and general overload of information online, we're bombarded with contradictory diet and weight-loss tips. It would take an iron will not to be affected by the noise all around us.

So how do we make sense of it all? Does fat make us fat, or is it healthy to follow a low-carb, high-fat regime, as in Atkins? Should we eat less protein; is sugar really a killer; and what about cholesterol, insulin and Omega 3, 6 and 9? Is our food acidic or alkaline; what's it doing to our glycaemic index? Should we fast for two days a week, as in the blockbuster 5:2 diet? Is it safe to ingest clay: will it really purify our insides? Should we be eating like werewolves (a diet based on the phases of the moon) or is it cavemen now?

On the subject of cavemen, I live with one. My boyfriend is a Paleo devotee, extolling the virtues of meat, fish, fowl, eggs, vegetables, healthy sources of fat like avocados, nuts and seeds, olive oil, fish oil and coconut oil. Based on the concept of foraging, hunter-gathering, and eating what our Paleolithic ancestors ate, the regime also eliminates sugar, wheat, trans-fats and industrialised Omega-6 fats, and contains little or no dairy. The Paleo case is that our species is simply not designed to cope with highly processed and high-calorie foods, so they cause havoc with our digestive systems. The first Paleo restaurant opened in London at the end of 2014; an indication of just how popular the movement has become.

My boyfriend gave me *The Primal Blueprint*, a book by Mark Sisson. Like the Paleo community, Sisson rejects traditional Western wisdom that grains and carbohydrates should form the basis of a balanced diet. He argues that our society's 'massive daily infusion of insoluble grain fibre' is at the root of obesity, heart disease, diabetes, inflammation, irritable bowel syndrome and countless other modern afflictions. According to Sisson, gluten and lectin in grains are dangerous, mess with our satiety hormones and send our insulin responses haywire.

So who's right? Are Sisson and his cavemen buddies right to demonise grains? Theirs is an extreme view, but it makes some sense. In the West we consume carbs and grains at almost every meal – toast, sandwiches, pasta, potatoes, rice, biscuits – and digestive complaints such as IBS and bloating are common. We've been told for decades that fibre is essential, and that we should eat plenty of 'roughage'. Until I learnt about the Paleo approach, I'd never even considered the fact that fibre is insoluble and our earliest ancestors didn't eat crops.

Paleo and *The Primal Blueprint* are straightforward in principle but harder in practice: most tasty things contain sugar or carbs. I've noticed that for all his Stone Age sympathies, my boyfriend rarely turns down croissants, tagliatelle or roast potatoes.

(In the interests of fairness, I should add that Mark Sisson is no diet-fascist. He advocates occasional treats – which he calls 'sensible vices' – on *The Primal Blueprint*, and believes that everyone should indulge from time to time without guilt. Fortunately, dark chocolate, cheese and wine are all 'sensible vices'!)

At the root of it all lies a more profound question: is life really worth living without delicious things to eat? Is being a caveman or cavewoman more important than satisfying your yearning for a plate of spaghetti carbonara?

As a vegetarian, who loves lentils, chickpeas, kidney beans and rice, I hope the cavemen are wrong. But I'm clearly not the only one who feels anxious. There is a lot of nutritional information out there, most of it contradictory. There are doctors, journalists and charlatans with miracle diets to peddle, and billion-dollar companies targeting us hard with their products. At some point, we have to make the choice to end the anxiety and just to eat what works for us, within reason: food which makes our bodies feel healthy, which won't make us gain or lose too much weight, which we can afford and which tastes good.

I've been much happier since I accepted there is no such thing as the perfect diet. Letting go of the anxiety I experienced around my own eating habits was liberating. Recovery, which at first I thought meant 'perfect recovery' is meaningless – good enough is just fine. I sensed all along that I'd probably never be totally anxiety-free around food, and that's fine too. Anyway, 'normal' is a slippery concept these days. It was a relief, gradually to realise that plenty of normal, healthy people have unusual eating habits too.

This came home to me last winter, while filming the latest series of *Supersize vs Superskinny*. I got an early train to Manchester, then a taxi to a small town near Rochdale. It was my first day with a new director, Helen, and a new assistant producer, Louise. I arrived at the leisure centre to meet the members of *Strictly Wheelchair Dancing* – an inspiring group of wheelchair users who challenge body image and disability issues through music, movement and dance.

Helen and Louise were inside setting up lights and rearranging the furniture. We got coffees and sat down to run through the filming schedule, and to get to know each other better.

Almost the first thing Helen said was: 'You should know I'm quite weird about food. I recently lost nearly seven stone – I was 19 stone – and I have strange habits. Anyway, if we're going to be working and travelling together, you'll see...'

And I did see. For the next few days we drove all over the north of England in our people carrier, ducking in and out of motorway superstores to grab breakfast, lunch and dinner on the road. Helen ate unusual things: raw tender-stem broccoli drenched in white wine vinegar, whole bags of raw carrots. She bought 25 g bags of cashew nuts, but only 25 g bags, no more and no less. 'If I get a bigger bag, I'll eat the entire thing – I can't just eat half and leave the rest. I know that's weird but it's the only way to control my bingeing.' Louise had her quirks too: large quantities of salmon at any time of the day and chilli flakes sprinkled on everything. They both carried sachets of seeds in their handbags – with my superfood powders, in hotels our breakfast table looked like the counter of a health food shop.

It was such a relief! Suddenly I didn't feel awkward any more. So what if I wanted a certain kind of bread (multi-seeded, high in omega-3) for lunch every day and a banana (not green) mid-afternoon? So what if I preferred to eat my Greek yogurt with a small silver (not plastic) spoon? It didn't make me abnormal – maybe eccentric or choosy, but not anorexic, not screwed up.

For so long I'd felt embarrassed about eating with others. Travelling, filming, living with Helen and Louise, I realised that there was nothing to be ashamed of. We were all eating different amounts of different food at different times, but we were all eating enough. We were healthy, happy, not overweight nor underweight, managing to live perfectly well despite our weird tastes. (Admittedly, the van smelt disgusting by the end of the week: vinegar, fish, chilli, banana skins...)

That's why I'm happier these days: because there is no such thing as the perfect diet, and there is probably no such thing as 'normal'. Recovery means accepting that mostly healthy is good enough, for most people, most of the time. It means learning to chill out about the whole thing.

And recovery is being able to cope when things go wrong on the food front: when your salad arrives, drenched in a creamy dressing, or the steamed vegetables are not 'just steamed' as requested, but swimming in butter. In the old days, that kind of unforeseen food event would have been calamitous for me. Nowadays, it's just a blip. When the low-fat yogurt is sold out, I'll wrinkle my nose and buy the regular version. Food fear no longer rules my life. Like anyone else, I have my preferences, but I can adapt. Letting go of the need to police my food so intensely has freed me to enjoy life more.

And now?

My boyfriend is in the kitchen 'slaving over a hot stove'. I'm lying in the bath, recovering from a long day walking in the Chilterns. The warm water soothes my tired muscles, and I'm looking forward to dinner and the first glass of wine. It strikes me that this is the happiest I've been for a long time.

'Something smells amazing,' I say, wandering into the kitchen. He's adding olive oil to a large pan and turns to smile at me. 'You're going to like this,' he says. 'Wild Camargue rice, asparagus, green beans, spinach, tomato sauce, lentils, kidney beans... '

After dinner and red wine, we indulge in a few squares of 90 per cent dark chocolate (remember, everyone needs 'sensible vices'). Why is this evening worth mentioning? Because it represents how far I've come. Allowing someone else to cook without hovering in the kitchen to monitor the ingredients, and then eating with complete enjoyment and zero anxiety. Eating without worrying about the fat content or asking for separate dishes. I know full well that my boyfriend adds excessive amounts of extra virgin olive oil. But that's all part of the fun.

Remember those emails from my father? He told me that enjoying and sharing food is part of a good relationship, and I was too deeply in denial to listen. But of course he was right.

Perhaps we could all allow ourselves to let go a little more and to relax around food. Looking around me, I see a lot of obsession with 'clean eating', with calorie burning and weight loss. I see a lot of women who are alarmingly underweight. Let's be honest, drinking a green juice when your body is crying out for a proper breakfast is miserable. Good nutrition is important, but so is happiness. Food is our basic fuel, it gives us the energy to function fully, and it's also pleasure. I'm not arguing we should over-indulge on processed 'junk', because plenty of 'virtuous' food is delicious, but I do think we should cut ourselves some slack. Are we going to live like this forever: fighting a battle between our natural hunger signals and our bathroom scales?

Life's too short to be on a never-ending diet. I've settled somewhere around the healthy-week, indulgent-weekend compromise (I'd call it 5:2 but that term has been hijacked by the bonkers fasting diet). In other words, eating healthily Monday to Friday, with loads of fruit and vegetables, protein and good fats, and then enjoying whatever I want at weekends: red wine, French cheese, dark chocolate, cake and second helpings of everything. Not excessive at weekends, but not restrictive during the week.

Caring about what you put in your body definitely matters, but so does nurturing your soul. If you're skipping meals or counting calories, if you can't enjoy bread or pasta, if sugar is the enemy, the whole business of eating becomes fraught with anxiety. There is a reason why *comfort* food is called that: sometimes cake is more comforting than kale. And here's the wonderful thing: when we learn to trust our bodies, to honour our hunger and to enjoy food again, diets and calorie counting become unnecessary. Your body, adequately fed, finds a natural balance. Not skinny or overweight; just the right size and shape for you. And when you give up guilt, punishment and deprivation, real food tastes fantastic.

Chapter Six

SUPERSIZE VS SUPERSKINNY

'Here are the ingredients for my special cereal mix.' Pauline opens the kitchen cupboards and unloads an assortment of packets and jars. 'Each evening I weigh out the oats, barley, grains and seeds, then I add skimmed milk and leave it to soak overnight. In the morning, I chop four or five different kinds of fruit into it: apricots, bananas, prunes, that type of thing. Then I add nuts, raisins and three tablespoons of fat-free yogurt on top. It takes me about an hour to prepare and another hour to eat it. Then I go to the gym to do an hour of weights, then an hour on the treadmill, until it's time to start measuring out the lunch ingredients...'

The woman in front of me is beautiful but ravaged, her skin etched with lines, her long blonde hair dry as straw. After we finish filming her kitchen routine she takes me aside and tells me more about how desperate her life with anorexia has been: 'I'm 59 years old now, and it feels like I've wasted the last 45 years.'

Throughout our time together, Pauline is warm and friendly and funny – you wouldn't think someone so 'normal' could have spent most of her life in such torment. Two hours to prepare and eat breakfast, another two hours over lunch, the same rigmarole for dinner, and in between nothing but a pointless, punishing exercise regime. No time for a partner or friends, and no social life to speak of. When I look at her crumbling teeth and nails, all I can think is: There but for the grace of God...

So what was I doing there? The interview with Pauline was for *Supersize vs Superskinny*: I was talking to sufferers with a wide range of eating disorders, exploring the latest research and investigating new treatments in the field.

You might think that would be the worst thing for someone who had suffered from anorexia – and you wouldn't be the only one. When I was first contacted by Endemol, the production company which makes *Supersize* for Channel 4, my family and friends thought I was mad even to consider it. 'Are you sure about this?' 'You don't want to get too involved in that world again, do you?' More troubling was the response of my psychiatrist: 'I have grave reservations about this Emma; it could be detrimental to your recovery.' After writing my column in *The Times* for three years, they all felt I needed some privacy back in my life. They were worried, too, that spending time with severely ill people could trigger me to start losing weight again.

I understood their concerns, of course, and I took them seriously. In the end, I decided to trust my instincts. The thing about recovery is that it's an ongoing process. It took strength to get healthy and it takes strength to stay healthy. I was excited by the challenge, and I wanted to test myself. If I wasn't robust enough to talk to others about their eating disorders, how could I call myself recovered?

And I believed it mattered to bring sensible coverage of anorexia and bulimia to mainstream TV. This thing we call 'disordered eating' is far more prevalent than the statistics might suggest. Almost everyone I meet has a story of their own food or weight concerns – men, women, old, young, even the sanest and most balanced among us. The participants in *Supersize* (from skinny to obese) were extreme examples, but we can all identify with unusual eating habits, a fear of fatness, a tendency to restrict, to reward or punish oneself, disliking one's own body, or feeling out of control around food. It doesn't matter what you look like on the outside, your size, weight or shape, anything can be going on inside.

We all know what we think of reality TV shows like *Supersize vs Superskinny* – or at least we all know the bad reputation they enjoy. They're hugely popular with viewers, but are frequently criticised for being sensationalist or exploitative.

In fact, *Supersize* was far more nuanced and interesting than I'd expected. If it's attacked for being shocking, it is – because they show many shocking realities. They show the reality of the morbidly obese, gruesome weight-related illnesses, even supersized mortuaries – but this is fact, not fiction. Setting aside the vocal critics, many viewers credit *Supersize* with shocking them into making positive, healthy changes to their diet and lifestyle. In that way, it's an important – if brutal – wake-up call about the causes and consequences of obesity.

My section focused on the opposite problem: those who eat too little rather than too much. Not only did this take me into a dizzying spectrum of sickness, secrecy and shame, it was also a journey of self-discovery. I had received countless letters and emails in response to my books, but writing was always a private act, anonymous. I had control of the boundaries. Television was an entirely new world: for the first time I was interviewing people about their eating disorders (and speaking about mine) on screen.

So why on earth would I get involved? I don't dream of a TV career – I've never even owned a television set. But in those initial conversations with Endemol, I began to believe that we could communicate something important about eating disorders, beyond the sensational or the simplistic 'shock' TV. Developing the films was a collaborative process: we decided together which areas to investigate, and I was given free rein with my interview scripts. As a former anorexic, I had a licence to ask the questions that others couldn't. Understandably, contributors felt more at ease, because I had been through the same thing. I was determined to be honest.

And I was. Filming wasn't entirely smooth: with any TV company the emphasis is on maximum visual impact. However, eating disorders are highly individual conditions, and the complexities of mental illness are not easily explained in a 10-minute documentary. There were moments when I had to put my foot down, to refuse to pursue an insensitive line of questioning, or to simplify in a way which might misrepresent the subject matter.

I also had to set clear boundaries around my personal life. While the production company wanted to include as much of my 'back-story' as possible, I was less keen. Why should my friends or family have to be involved in a television programme just because I was? This was a good lesson in asserting myself and in learning to compromise. It was also a valuable reminder that in our working lives, our personal lives, and especially on social media, we all need to be clear about our boundaries. In the new digital, always-connected universe, our gadgets and devices risk blurring the lines between private and public. Just as I insisted on keeping my home life away from the cameras, I think we could all benefit from keeping some areas off-limits. This can be as simple as switching off work emails at home, not posting family (or baby) photos online, or not discussing personal problems in the office. As we're increasingly sharing (many of us over-sharing) online, there is something special about having a space, a relationship, family time, to oneself. My home is the place I run to when everything gets too much; I needed to keep that sanctuary to myself.

These were minor niggles. On the whole, filming *Supersize* was a positive experience. I remember the excitement of watching the first show, my boyfriend refilling my wine glass as fast as I could gulp it down. I quickly became as competitive as the production team about viewing figures: did we outdo Nigella's new show? Were we trending on Twitter?

When that first show aired I found myself thinking back to Pauline and the others I had met.

There was Margaret, a woman of 65 who had been fit and healthy all her life before developing 'late onset' anorexia. What had started as a diet in her 50s, as a response to the natural weight gain of the menopause, quickly became an addiction. She lost more than half her body weight and around 6 inches in height, due to the bone wasting of osteoporosis. Her house was full of photographs of her grandchildren, and she cried as she told me she was now too frail to take them to the playground. She showed me some holiday snaps from when she was in her 30s and 40s, a normal woman with normal curves: not remotely 'fat'. She had no previous history of mental illness, until the anorexia had taken hold. When I hugged her goodbye I thought she was going to snap in two.

There was Daniel, a handsome young man in his 20s. Filming in a canal-side pub in north London, he told me how close he had come to death. 'Last year I reached a breaking point. Between Christmas and New Year I took around 1,000 laxatives. I just stayed in, eating and taking these pills, only going out to buy more pills, then eating and throwing up… My body began to fail. I realised, one afternoon, staggering between my bedroom and bathroom, I was having a heart attack.'

I visited Amy, a young mother in Walsall, chain-smoking as she told me about her two pregnancies. She was so underweight and weak during her first labour that she was almost unable to push her baby out, and she and the baby nearly died. When her two young children came home from nursery, we filmed her making their supper – pasta with a tin of tomato sauce. The director filmed Amy's special cupboard full of small bottles of 'Ensure' (a meal replacement drink) and chocolate biscuits. Some days, she said, that was all she was able to eat. I caught her two-year-old daughter gazing at us as we discussed her illness, and I wondered what it was like growing up with a mummy who didn't eat. Although Amy was still not well, she was determined to stay out of hospital and bring up her children. She told me that they were her 'little miracles' and the greatest motivation for her to recover.

Back in London I interviewed a young man, Sam, founder of Men Get Eating Disorders Too, a campaigning charity he set up during his own battle with bulimia. The organisation challenges common misconceptions about male eating disorders and sexuality, as Sam explained: 'Most people assume that eating disorders are predominantly female conditions, and therefore that men who get them are gay – they're somehow more feminine, concerned with their body, weight, etc.' In fact, there is no evidence that disordered eating is more prevalent in gay men, although they may well be more hidden among straight men. Additionally, the medical profession, teachers and parents are more alert for signs of eating disorders in girls and women, so the condition in boys and men often goes undiagnosed and untreated. Male eating disorders are also rife in sports which depend on strict weight categories, such as boxing or horse-racing. Sam's organisation promotes awareness of the issues faced by men of all ages and body types, irrespective of their sexuality, and campaigns for improved treatment.

In Newcastle I spent time with Tracy, the mother of a young woman called Jay. Jay had died from anorexia only a few weeks before, aged 25. Much as Tracy was keen to share her story, at times those interviews were almost unbearable; her grief was so raw. 'I held my Jay when she took her first breath and I held her when she took her last,' she told me. 'She died right here in our little kitchen.' I sat on Jay's bed with her two sisters as they showed me her clothes and diaries. Her mother had a memory box of belongings: her sparkly pink iPhone, her hairclips, make-up... Before we left, they took me to her graveside. It brought it home to me: this is where it ends. Anorexia kills. It was incredibly brave of Jay's family to talk about her death.

They were proud of her life and determined that something meaningful should come out of their loss.

In Amsterdam I interviewed a bubbly Dutch woman called Jessica. She told me about a new kind of online treatment programme she was using for her binge-eating disorder. The website (www.interapy.nl) was manned by trained staff 24 hours a day, and she could log on whenever she was tempted to start bingeing. Later, in a riverside boutique we filmed Jessica teaching me one of her techniques for self-acceptance and body confidence: 'You take off all your clothes and start by looking yourself directly in the eye.' We both stood in front of full-length mirrors, clothed of course. 'You tell yourself nice things about your face, your smile. Then you move on to your shoulders and arms. You appreciate the creamy skin, or the freckles, you say nice things. Then you move down throughout your body, your breasts, your thighs, appreciating every part of you.' We laughed, both feeling self-conscious in front of the cameras. Jessica was certainly 'plus size' – she stood well over 6 foot in her socks and weighed around 18 stone – but her size was magnificent, as was her smile, and flaming red cropped hair. It was very moving, seeing a woman who had binged and dieted, despised and damaged herself for decades, speaking this self-acceptance out loud.

And Jessica's exercise holds a lesson for us all. She may be 'plus size' in strict fashion terms, but why should we allow clothes manufacturers to decide our body shapes? To the outside world, she was striking and stylish, with stunning blue eyes and a knockout smile. That day, standing in front of the mirror in an Amsterdam boutique, I learnt that there are so many words for beautiful and so many body types – from petite to willowy, athletic to curvaceous, boyish to hourglass. Every one of us has a body to be proud of.

The experience was all the more powerful because of the years Jessica had spent loathing herself. She had fought hard for inner peace and physical self-acceptance. Although her road had been rockier than most, it's a reminder that the way we see our own bodies is highly subjective, and often negative or inaccurate. I could see that Jessica looked fantastic, just as you can see the beauty in your friends, sisters or children. Why is it so hard to see the beauty in ourselves?

Maybe we should include the occasional mirror session in our own lives. Rather than buying clothes which hide our 'lumps', or make-up which conceals our 'flaws', maybe we should strip and stand in front of the mirror, and appreciate the amazing, unique parts of our body which are ours alone.

I also interviewed specialists who explained the scientific facts: Professor Bryan Lask, a high-profile neuroscientist who is pioneering the brain scans that show anorexia may be an actual neurological dysfunction. I interviewed Dr Nadia Micali at UCL, who investigates pregnancy in women with eating disorders. She was enlightening – if frightening – on the serious damage an underweight mother can cause to her unborn baby by being at a low weight.

Professor Lask's brain research is vital to the understanding of anorexia, a disorder that is often characterised as a lifestyle 'choice'. Because of the modern obsession with thinness, it's seen as an extreme diet, driven by vanity and the pursuit of the body beautiful. Professor Lask has turned this debate on its head, demonstrating that there may well be neurological differences in the brains of sufferers, even a genetic pre-disposition to developing anorexia. His MRI scans indicate that the insula, a part of the brain which plays a crucial role in healthy brain function, appears to shrink in cases of severe anorexia. More worrying still, he showed that the underactive insula may never recover.

Dr Micali's studies on pregnancy and eating disorders are equally thought-provoking. Her research suggests that the unborn babies of underweight women tend to be significantly smaller than those of healthy-weight women. Her findings highlight the risk of major adverse outcomes for the expectant mother during pregnancy and birth, and complications for the baby in later life.

The work of both Professor Lask and Dr Micali has the potential to transform the treatment of eating disorders. Many *Supersize* viewers told us that they had encountered a lack of understanding from the medical community, psychiatrists, family and friends; another reason why research like this really matters.

Meeting these experts during the filming of the series gave me greater insight into my own experiences. The truth about eating disorders is unpleasant, even alarming, but it's also a weapon with which to fight the illness. The greatest spur in my own recovery was focusing on my health; armed with information, I began to set clear goals for weight gain and good nutrition. It's essential that anyone suffering from anorexia or bulimia comprehends the causes and consequences of their condition; that they understand the devastating damage they can do; and finally, that they have access to the specialist support they need.

If dealing with a mental illness is challenging, how about dealing with it on top of a severe physical disability? When filming the latest series I was keen that we should cover eating disorders and disability – a problem rarely explored in the media.

Think of all the 'normal' teenage issues you faced growing up: fitting in at school, looking attractive, the hang-ups we have about our bodies, the crazy diets we try, how we feel about sex and relationships… Then imagine being disabled and multiply those hang-ups by a million. As my friend Sarah said during our interview for *Supersize*: 'We fit the profile for an eating disorder perfectly. And no one even thinks about it.'

Until I met Sarah, I hadn't thought about these issues either. She had written to me a few months after the publication of *An Apple a Day* and, along with a few other readers, we ended up meeting for coffee in London. Sarah is in her late 20s, lives in Southampton and works as a learning resource manager at the university. As well as a long history of anorexia and bulimia, she also has cerebral palsy.

Witnessing the physical challenges Sarah faces, from negotiating King's Cross in heavy snow to finding space in the coffee shop for her wheelchair, not to mention the endless infections and medical emergencies, the stigma, the staring, the 24/7 experience of cerebral palsy, filled me with admiration. I won't call her 'brave' – I know Sarah would prefer not to be disabled – and her bravery goes without saying. Rather it's her determination to get on with things that impresses me. She has her career, she has a colourful love life (her last boyfriend cheated on her so she replaced him pronto!) she travels and tweets and wears beautiful outfits. Her muscle control is virtually nil: she has a full-time carer to wash and feed her, even in our cafe get-togethers her carer has to come along, but she doesn't let it get in the way of taking part in life.

It was my friendship with Sarah that opened my eyes to the realities of having an eating disorder while being profoundly disabled. Why had I never thought about this before? Perhaps we look at someone in a wheelchair and only see the disability. Perhaps we only see the wheelchair. But when you think about it, a young person in a wheelchair faces major body image issues. If, like Sarah, a carer is feeding them, they face huge control issues too. If they're paralysed, their caloric needs are very different to those of others. They can't exercise easily, they can't buy their own food. They cannot even stand on a pair of bathroom scales.

Imagine being a 15-year-old girl, going through puberty, and having a parent still undressing you to give you a bath. Imagine developing bulimia and having your carer take you to the bathroom. Imagine trying to buy fashionable clothes and having a completely different body size and shape to all your female friends. Imagine having boys you fancy look right through you because you're in a wheelchair. Imagine going to the school disco in that chair.

And then, you get sick. Imagine doctors ignoring your mental health because you've got cerebral palsy. Imagine finally opening up to your consultant and being told, as Sarah was, 'don't you think you have enough physical problems already?' as though you'd chosen to develop an eating disorder. Imagine being driven to the local veterinary surgery to be lifted on to the scales and weighed like an animal.

Sarah experienced all this, and worse.

After the show I received tweets and emails from many others facing similar difficulties. This message stood out:

> *Like Sarah, I was born with cerebral palsy. This means that I can't walk and I use a wheelchair the majority of the time. I also have epilepsy as a result of the brain damage that occurs in the condition. As well as my physical difficulties, I suffer from anorexia nervosa, anxiety and depression. I was diagnosed with anorexia by my GP at the age of 16 after restricting, over-exercising (I'm a 1,000m swimmer despite the fact I can't walk), purging and hiding food. This was largely ignored by my consultant because 'there is no way you can engage in true anorexic behaviour and not walk'. Basically I could lose weight without my professionals really knowing or caring.*

Before *Supersize*, there had been almost no media coverage of eating disorders and disability. There is still very little information and treatment available. So when people criticise the programme for insensitive or inaccurate reporting, I ask them to watch it first.

Of all the patients and experts we filmed for *Supersize*, there is one who will stick in my mind forever.

It was a cold winter's morning and we were standing around in the foyer of a hotel in central London. The director set up lights and cameras, we drank coffee and went over the interview notes; the assistant producer rang to say that she was on her way from the airport with our participant. Finally a black taxi drew up. Slowly, tortuously, Valeria began to get out. As our eyes met, I was filled with sadness and pity.

Before I met Valeria, I'd been sceptical. This label, 'the thinnest woman in the world' was something cooked up by the TV company, surely. Who decides who is the world's thinnest woman? But as she made her way painfully out of the taxi I realised it could well be true. I doubt there is anyone thinner alive.

I've seen very sick patients in specialist eating-disorder units before, and I've seen old people destroyed by cancer. I've seen the posters of Isabelle Caro, a model who died of anorexia in 2010. But I have never in my life seen anyone like Valeria. The shock of being around her is hard to describe.

She is a medical miracle. Or perhaps I should say a medical mystery, because there is nothing miraculous about it. I know of many people who have died from anorexia weighing a lot more than Valeria does. There is no way, really, she should be alive. She refuses to admit that she has severe anorexia. She claims she's 'mentally recovered, but with a few physical complications'. One doctor I spoke to told me 'her body mass index isn't classified as underweight – it's off the scale'.

During the course of a week, I didn't see Valeria eat a single thing. Once she took a tiny sip of diet coke, but then left the rest: remember, diet coke contains nearly one calorie per 330 ml can. The catering team at Valeria's hotel had been briefed in advance and brought in specially prepared sashimi for her every evening, although I'm not sure if she ate any of it.

Valeria's health is so precarious and her ability to function so curtailed, that we were severely restricted by health and safety regulations. Getting in and out of taxis was a laborious process, walking was slow and shaky, stairs were near impossible. Her body temperature is so low that she requires constant heat of around 30°C. The assistant producer had to ring ahead to cafes and shops, asking them to turn the heating right up, and to close all windows and doors. When she arrived in London (after weeks of delays and cancellations) she was en route to a cruise in Mexico: the winter months in Europe are too cold for her.

As well as requesting full-on central heating, the assistant producer had to try to clear locations of the general public. The reaction to her was appalling: one scene, where we walked a few metres along Tottenham Court Road from a taxi into the Planet Organic cafe, people stared at her in the street, jaws dropping, openly shocked.

I've come into contact with many people while filming *Supersize* – some who are physically emaciated, mentally unwell, nervous or suspicious, but it's always been rewarding in the end. Talking to people, sharing their life stories, you find the warm, human being underneath. Not so with Valeria. In our first interview she blocked, ignored and finally banned a growing list of topics of what 'I will not discuss'. I wondered why she had agreed to take part, since she refused to admit that she was sick and she refused to discuss weight, hospitals, treatment or eating. Anorexia hasn't simply wrecked her body: it has also damaged her head and her heart.

I shouldn't be surprised – the brain is a muscle like the rest of the body and it wastes away as the body starves. Valeria is a terrible warning to any young woman who might think there is anything desirable or glamorous about anorexia.

I hope I'm not judging Valeria too harshly. Looking back, I can understand why she is so hostile. Everywhere she goes, people stare. My illness was less extreme than hers, but I still remember those looks of pity. They make you very defensive.

When we look at others with shock or distaste, we should remember how this makes them feel. Spending time with Valeria, Sarah and the others, reminded me of the scrutiny they face on a daily basis. As if the illness or disability itself wasn't enough of a challenge, they're also dealing with constant, unwanted attention from the outside world, merely for the way they look. Accepting ourselves means accepting others too. Letting go of judgement, respecting the abilities and disabilities, the strengths and limitations, of others, would surely make all our lives richer in the process.

At times it was a strain, spending long filming days with participants who simply did not, could not, eat. But overall, *Supersize* sealed the deal on my own recovery. Being plunged back into the world of starvation, sadness and eating disorders tested and then strengthened my resolve. It reminded me how destructive anorexia was, and how far I've come. It enabled me to let go of the past.

Chapter Seven

THE GIRL WITH THE
APPLE TATTOO

The deed is done. After years of wanting to get myself inked I've finally gone and done it.

Body art is everywhere these days, but it wasn't always so. When I was a teenager I didn't know anyone who had a tattoo. Now they're commonplace across all social classes, genders and ages. A recent US study found that 36 per cent of Americans aged 18–29, 24 per cent of those aged 30–40 and 15 per cent of those aged 41–51 have a tattoo.

Here in the UK, *Vogue* reported in April 2014 that a third of women aged 16–44 now have a tattoo. My parents forbade me even to get my ears pierced until the age of 18, and I can still remember the furore when my younger sister came home with a silver ring through her belly button. In my 20s I considered a tattoo, but wasn't sure what to get. When I think back over the unsuitable boyfriends' initials I might have chosen, the oh-so-profound song lyrics, or smiley faces, I'm glad I didn't have the courage – until now.

So what changed? I blame social media... I had made a rash promise on Twitter, possibly after a glass of wine, that when I reached a certain number of followers I'd get a tattoo. It seemed like a good idea at the time – and I hate to renege on a promise! Twitter friends (i.e. strangers) egged me on, tweeting me photos of their own body art, and the idea gained momentum.

As well as the Twitter challenge, there was something else. I had reached a turning point and I wanted to mark it in some way. I was letting go of the past and entering a new phase of my life. A tattoo seemed like a way of honouring this transition – inscribing it forever on my body. This body had not been well, physically or emotionally, for a long time. I was coming out of that dark tunnel and emerging into the light. I wanted to acknowledge my rebirth and celebrate it.

Tattooing may be experiencing a modern-day resurgence, but of course it's an ancient art. Evidence of ritual tattooing goes back as early as BC6000, in cultures across Southeast Asia, Africa, New Zealand, the Americas, Europe and even Iron Age Britain. Tattoos have been used to signal rites of passage, identity of tribes, and beliefs; they have been adopted as symbolic markers for centuries. Any permanent mark on our skin is significant; childhood nicks and scrapes, lasting wounds from injury, caesarean scars; events in our lives etched into our skin. Perhaps tattoos come from the same impulse, that human desire to hold a moment in time; to stamp ourselves with a motto or symbol we find meaningful; to pledge ourselves to someone we love, or to pay tribute to someone who has died, to carry that person with us, literally, on our bodies.

Getting a tattoo carries a certain risk, but it's also a sign of confidence. Maybe I'd regret it in years to come, but so what if I did? I had been far too controlled for far too long. Why not do something fun – quite possibly foolish – just for the hell of it?

The first step was to work out where this inking would take place. I know where to go in London for a decent haircut, manicure, even ear piercing – but when it came to tattoos I was clueless. I had visions of dodgy joints in seedy Soho backstreets, filled with men in motorbike leathers with ponytails, dirty needles everywhere. My priority was hygiene and safety, with someone who knew what they were doing. The financial cost seemed irrelevant: this tattoo would be forever and I was willing to pay for it. Obviously, I hit Google: I began researching 'posh tattoos'.

Eventually I found a groovy little studio near me in Hoxton. A beautiful Japanese woman called Kanae showed me various designs and told me about the philosophy of traditional Japanese body art: they believe that tattoos are important personal items that will remain on our bodies forever. This way of thinking stems from the legacy of Japanese 'shokunin' or craftsmen, who devote 100 per cent attention to every single piece they create, no matter how big or small. She told me: 'We're interested in creating works that stand the test of time and bring the wearer a sense of happiness and well-being for the rest of their life.'

Kanae learnt her craft under the tutelage of Makoto, a tattooist in Shizuoka, Japan. I was reassured by her serious approach: she was a proper artist, with a proper philosophy; this would be a spiritual act, not just a Twitter stunt! I noticed that her own body decoration was tasteful and well executed – she had some exquisite little stars around her fingers, which I was quite tempted to copy.

In the end, I decided to stick with my own symbol. Kanae sketched it on paper, and we discussed the size and colour. I would pay half the amount as a deposit, and she would design the tattoo itself. The night before I'd reached the requisite number of followers on Twitter, so I had no excuse: we set a date for the following week. Even as I paid up, even as the day of the inking drew near, I wasn't sure I'd really go through with it.

Tattoos used to be associated with sailors, Hell's Angels bikers and pirates, but in recent years they have become thoroughly mainstream. Here in the UK they increasingly span the ages and social classes. Samantha Cameron, the wife of our current Prime Minister, has a discreet dolphin tattoo on her ankle. Women have gone for tattoos in a big way: among the countless high-profile female fans are Sienna Miller, Angelina Jolie and Victoria Beckham.

Older celebrities are at it too: the actress Felicity Kendal and the broadcaster David Dimbleby are among those getting inked in later life. Kendal, in her late 60s, has a moon and two feathers on her calf, a star on her foot and a turtle on her shoulder. She says she prefers tattoos to Botox on older women – and explains her decision: 'I'm doing it now because I know where the wrinkly bits are.' Dimbleby, the host of BBC's *Question Time*, acquired his first tattoo in 2013 at the age of 75, a scorpion on his shoulder.

Understandably, those who took the risk back when it was still risqué, express annoyance at how normal tattoos have become. The actress Helen Mirren has a native American symbol meaning 'equal but opposite' on her left thumb, and she's amusing in interviews about how this came about: 'I was very, very drunk. It was a very, very long time ago... I decided to get a tattoo because it was the most shocking thing I could think of doing. And now I'm utterly disgusted and shocked because it's become completely mainstream, which is unacceptable to me.'

Lady Judy Steel, wife of the former Liberal Party leader David Steel, got a leaping pink jaguar tattoo to celebrate her 70th birthday a few years ago. She snuck off to a parlour in Selkirk without telling her husband and paid £30 for the three-inch tattoo (cheap, compared with London prices!). When he first saw it, Lord Steel apparently said: 'I assume that's a transfer.' Explaining her decision, Lady Steel said: 'It was very liberating because it was sort of proving that you're never too old to do mad things.' Like Felicity Kendal, she chose a less-wrinkly body part: 'It's on my shoulder – a bit of me that doesn't show the wear and tear of all the years spent enjoying food and wine.'

Common to all these stories is that expression of confidence and fun. Getting a tattoo in older age is unexpected, even a little bit shocking. It challenges the accepted notion of physical ageing as a period of decline, and for women, increasing invisibility. In a society that values smooth, perky flawlessness so highly, we are brainwashed into believing that the elderly body is not beautiful. We cover up as we age, we camouflage the blemishes and wrinkles, we hide away the saggy bits. Even if we don't feel it ourselves, we are reminded (by the media) that the mature form is not fit for public display.

In our youth-obsessed culture, getting a tattoo seems a wonderful way to decorate one's own body: a place which has lived through six, seven or eight decades, which has worked and played, travelled, given birth, survived illness, loss, and the slings and arrows of everyday life. Why not celebrate the timeworn physique?

Whatever your age, the placement of a tattoo still needs careful consideration. Kendal's choice, her shoulder, seems relatively safe. Among the young, the craze is increasingly for highly visible tattoos: where upper arms and shoulders used to be the most popular areas, now it's all about necks, lower arms and legs. This trend is reflected in younger celebrities, such as the singer Rihanna who has at least 19 tattoos, including stars cascading from her neck and down her back, and Roman numerals on her shoulder. She had the words 'rebelle fleur' inked on to her neck (which provoked an amusing debate online: for grammatical correctness, surely it should be 'fleur rebelle'?). She also has 'never a failure, always a lesson' tattooed backwards just below her collarbone, so she can read it in the mirror. Rihanna's BFF, the model Cara Delevingne, also has a taste for visible tattoos, including a lion's head on her index finger and the motto 'Don't worry, be happy' beneath her breasts.

Delevingne has referred in interviews to a 'tattoo addiction'. She acquired ten of her tattoos in the space of six months, all of which were feverishly documented and analysed by the media. The One Direction boy-band singer Harry Styles entered the public consciousness as an ink-free teen; he now has an estimated 50 tattoos (his torso is quite a sight). It's intriguing to watch young celebrities making these permanent choices and to consider how they will feel about them in years to come.

The singer Amy Winehouse was heavily tattooed, with anchors, topless pin-up girls, horseshoes, hearts, birds, musical notes and a Native American feather. She even had the name of her ex-husband, Blake, tattooed above her heart. Winehouse tragically died in 2011, aged 27, so we can't know how she would have felt about those youthful markings as an old lady.

My tattooist told me she regularly has teenagers requesting tattoos on their face and hands. I was reassured that she refuses to ink anyone under the age of 18, and would never tattoo anyone on their face or hands, no matter what their age. This question of visibility is becoming increasingly important: like those celebrities, it's a choice we make which could last for the rest of our lives. Ask yourself, where do you expect to see tattoos? Would they be acceptable on your GP, your MP, your children's primary school teacher?

In 2012 the Metropolitan Police issued the following ban to its serving officers: 'Tattoos on the face, or visible above a collar line, or on the hands are no longer permitted. All other tattoos must be covered. It will be a requirement, by the Commissioner, that all officers and police staff with existing tattoos defined as "visible" must register such tattoos as a formal written declaration to their line manager... '

Registering tattoos? Making formal written declarations? It sounds quite draconian, but the Met aren't the only large UK employer forced to confront this question. Among others are the Armed Forces and the National Health Service. There is no official NHS policy on tattoos, instead it varies from trust to trust. NHS Wales, for example, issues this guidance: 'It is recognised that tattoos and other body decoration have become prevalent in society. However, staff will be asked to cover up excessive/potentially offensive tattoo designs that it is judged are not in line with the spirit of this policy.'

The British Army has also introduced guidance on tattoos: one of the frequently asked questions on their recruitment website is: 'Can I join the Army with a tattoo?' The answer is generally yes, unless a tattoo is 'offensive, obscene or racist'. Small, non-offensive tattoos are deemed acceptable for soldiers, depending on how visible they are.

Is banning visible tattoos an infringement of our fundamental human rights, or a sensible measure to ensure that staff look presentable? Most workplaces, both in the public and private sector, have basic requirements for clean uniform or clothing, well-kempt hair, neat beards or moustaches, and general standards of hygiene and tidiness. Many health and social care employers even recommend the use of 'light deodorant' and ask staff to keep make-up 'to a minimum'. While our appearance is our own business, it seems it's also the business of our employers.

Of course tattoos are not intrinsically dirty or unhygienic, but what if the symbol or the wording is offensive to others? Should we ban swastikas and swear words but allow dolphins and poetry? What if an individual was working with elderly people in a care home, and a prominent tattoo was perceived as aggressive or frightening? There's no doubt that the realm of self-expression – body piercing, tattoos, even the wearing of religious symbols – is a minefield.

Hands, arms and necks are one thing, but some go a lot further. Thinking about the body parts people get inked is eye-watering: eyelids, inner lips, soles of feet, tongue or boob (known as a tattoob). The Internet is heaving with bizarre tattoos: the computer geeks with 'Ctrl Alt Del' keys decorating their ankles, the woman with the caffeine molecule emblazoned across her back, an obese man with the logos of his favourite fast-food outlets (McDonald's, Pizza Hut, KFC, Burger King) across his swollen stomach, lovers' and ex-lovers' names on armpits, genitals, chessboards on faces, sometimes witty, sometimes horrific, always extreme. Online you'll also find more disturbing examples of body art – full-face skulls being ripped open, flesh being unzipped to reveal the muscles and gore beneath, exposed brains and gruesome zombies. An old man with a lacy bra and panties inked on to his sagging body, a young woman with SLUT branded across her buttocks. What stories lie behind these tattoos?

One of the world's most tattooed individuals is Tom Leppard from the Isle of Skye. Also known as Scotland's 'Leopard Man', his body is almost entirely covered with a leopard-skin design. The only untattooed areas on the 80 year old are inside his ears and between his toes.

You don't need to go as far as the 'Leopard Man' to elicit disapproval. Some people believe that all tattoos are irredeemably vulgar. For others (my parents included) tattoos simply don't make sense. It's interesting how polarising body art can be. In 2012, the *Daily Telegraph* asked a range of female media commentators for their views. Emma Soames, editor-at-large of *Saga* magazine, didn't pull her punches: 'Over tattoos, the world divides into two camps – "body art" versus "tramp stamp". I am firmly in the tramp-stamp corner. I've never had one, never considered having one and never will. Indeed, I regard my greatest triumph of mothering as having kept my daughter out of tattoo parlours.'

(If I were her daughter and read that, I'd know exactly how to rebel!)

For all Soames' horror of the 'tramp stamp', in fact, history tells a different story. The tattoo can be a symbol of privilege. In 1862, the Prince of Wales, later King Edward VII, had a Jerusalem cross tattooed on his arm on a visit to the Holy Land. He was rumoured to mark his mistresses with a snake tattoo around the wrist (a form of branding one's cattle). His sons, the Duke of Clarence and the Duke of York, visited Japan in 1882 and both returned with dragons tattooed on their arms. Tattoos could also be found on members of the Russian royal family, including Peter the Great, Catherine the Great and Nicholas II; and Austro-Hungarian Archduke Franz Ferdinand, whose assassination sparked the First World War, also sported a tattoo.

The author, former MP and media controversialist Louise Mensch was typically outspoken on that *Daily Telegraph* question: 'Tattoos are horrendous... There's nothing attractive about them. Employers hate them. The sight of one ruins a working suit or evening dress... Tattoos are an attempt to freeze a moment in aspic; to have permanence in a body that changes, grows, adapts. They are regarded as low-class. And rightly so.'

I was amused by Mensch's strident condemnation of any of us pathetic enough to seek 'permanence in a body that changes, grows, adapts'. Only a few months later on *Newsnight* she confessed to having had a facelift: 'I had a little tightening in my face for maintenance.' Call me crazy, but I consider Mensch's facelift more extreme – and invasive – than a simple tattoo.

Extreme or not, there is evidence the backlash, sorry tatt-lash, against tattoos is spreading. The radio and TV presenter Fearne Cotton who has 11 tattoos recently admitted: 'There may be one or two I regret.' If she, or any of us, do come to regret our body art, the technology is evolving that may one day erase them forever.

As the demand for tattoos rises, so does the demand for reversal. More and more tattoo-removal salons are opening up across the UK, with some industry experts saying it will soon be as straightforward as going for a manicure or a haircut.

Techniques are improving all the time, and have undoubtedly moved on from the older, traditional methods, which failed to remove multi-pigmented colours from tattoos (greens, blues and blacks can be problematic). Dermabrasion acted like a sanding machine, resulting in damage to skin pigment, pale patches and even raised keloid scars. Now, advanced laser procedures are used to shatter ink into tiny dust-like particles, which are absorbed into the body. However, tattoo removal remains expensive and time-consuming. It's also extremely painful and the end result is far from guaranteed. As one tattooist puts it: 'You wouldn't get married thinking, *I can always get divorced*, and it's the same with body art – you shouldn't rely on the get-out clause.'

Many beauty brands now produce ultra-thick professional camouflage foundation to enable people to conceal tattoos. This may be fine for models on fashion shoots with a team of dedicated make-up artists, but in reality it's hard to keep them properly concealed. (As an experiment I dabbed a blob of foundation on my tattoo and bingo, it was invisible – but within hours it had rubbed off on to my clothes.)

True devotees don't get their tatts removed to restore their skin to its natural state, but rather to make way for something new! Sion Smith, the editor of *Skin Deep*, Britain's leading tattoo magazine, admits to making mistakes, including a huge tribal pattern he had done when he was a music journalist. 'I'm about to have it lasered away, although I'm going to have something done in its place. You never get clean skin back, just a canvas for another tattoo.'

I find this use of the term 'canvas' fascinating. Many people who are heavily inked clearly see their bodies as art: their skin a canvas on which to record people, places, emotions and experiences. Whenever I meet someone with a tattoo I ask about the stories behind them.

If you don't want to commit permanently, or you're not sure what to get, there are temporary techniques available. I remember some years ago while travelling in Spain I got a small yin-yang transfer on my shoulder. Like a holiday romance, it was fun for a few weeks, without the lifelong responsibility. Temporary tatts allow us to try out different symbols and positioning, to dip our toe into the waters of self-expression, to see what works on our bodies before making a commitment.

One celebrity who committed herself big-time is Cheryl (now Fernandez-Versini, formerly Cole), singer and former member of the pop group Girls Aloud. There are tattoos, and there are *tattoos*. In 2013, she unveiled her tenth piece of body art: entwined red roses completely covering her lower back and both buttocks. Her tattoo artist Instagrammed it during 'some intense tattoo sessions', and reported that despite the pain, Cheryl was 'as tough as nails'. This floral montage covers up an earlier butterfly design on the small of her back – although this seems like a hammer to crack a nut, as it now encompasses a significant section of her lower body.

Cheryl's former band mate Sarah Harding also has a prominent tattoo: a huge phoenix inked across her shoulder blades, along with the motto, 'Don't be bitter, glitter'.

It seems contradictory – and sometimes alarming – to see such flawless young women (and men) choosing such radical, disfiguring body art, stark symbols inked on to these otherwise 'perfect' forms. Psychiatrists have suggested that compulsive tattooing (and body piercing) may represent a cry for help, an attempt to externalise inner turmoil. One cannot deny the parallels with self-harm, in which people cut themselves to relieve the suffering they feel inside. Remember, this is not a shaved head or a bright pink wig: these tattoos last. When Delevingne refers to a 'tattoo addiction', should we take this seriously? And when an individual seems unable to stop tattooing themselves, are they trying to communicate something which is more than skin-deep?

The procedure itself also has disturbing parallels with cutting and injecting. Many people admit they find it strangely addictive: a friend with several sizable tattoos says he actually finds the pain of the needle 'cathartic'.

My tattoo wasn't a cry for help – if anything, it was the opposite. I was affirming my own recovery; despite the fact that it started as a Twitter dare, this would be a private symbol of health and renewed self-belief. So I definitely didn't want anything visible: no arms, wrists or ankles. I tried to imagine myself as a dignified old lady in evening dress and a tattoo didn't fit into that picture, so no shoulders either. Nor did I want a tattoo on my lower back, which would reveal itself in low-cut jeans. No tummies or breasts: I remember seeing a woman in a magazine with a circle of daisies around her navel, which then became irrevocably stretched during pregnancy. In the end I chose my right hip, a body part which will never be visible unless I'm wearing a bikini on the beach, or I take to nudism or pole dancing.

T-day arrived. I woke up and told my boyfriend I'd changed my mind. At breakfast I changed it back again. Arriving at the studio I had to sign a form consenting to 'permanent alteration of my appearance' (in my state of heightened anxiety this wording seemed sinister). After that things are a bit vague. I remember lying down while the tattooist set to work and thinking it would all be fine. Then came appalling agony, as if someone was carving into my hip with a scalpel. I knew it was a needle, not an actual blade, but I couldn't bring myself to look. It went on for nearly an hour while I gritted my teeth, tiny beads of sweat on my forehead, praying for it to be over.

I thought I had a decent pain threshold – I don't mind blood, injections or needles – but getting tattooed was far worse than I'd been expecting. Several people have since told me that tattoos hurt most on non-fleshy areas of the body. Others have helpfully said: 'Oh, you should have taken a couple of Nurofen Plus beforehand'.

Well, I had no painkillers. As Kanae drilled into my hip bone, Miae worked away on a middle-aged man on the other side of the studio. He was having two massive tattoo 'sleeves' on his arms joined across his back: soon his entire torso would be covered in snakes, dragons and other inky swirls. Between whimpers, I asked him how he could stand the pain. 'You get used to it, love. I think I must be hooked! It'll be weeks before this is finished – then I'll get started on my legs,' he said, cheerily. All I could think was: how does anyone get addicted to *this*?

Finally it was over. My wound, sorry tattoo, was wrapped in cling film, like a raw chunk of meat, and I was given instructions on how to keep it clean. What I hadn't expected was the bleeding involved: the needle injects the ink into the skin and the blood mixes with the coloured ink, resulting in a seeping, ugly mess.

That was an awful day. I limped around like a wounded animal, my breathing shallow and ragged. I needed soft fabric against my hip, but it hurt to change my jeans for tracksuit bottoms. It hurt like hell getting on and off my bike. I stood in line at the pharmacy clutching a tube of Bepanthen, the nappy rash ointment they recommend for tattoo aftercare. It even hurt to reach into my bag for my wallet. I dreaded going to bed that night: would I ever be able to lie on my right side again?

I forced myself to change the sodden dressing and tried not to look at this foolish thing I'd done. I emailed my parents that blood was gushing from my side – OK, a slight exaggeration – to which my beloved father replied: 'You must have taken leave of your senses Emma. It's no good asking me to drive you to A&E with self-inflicted wounds. Take some paracetamol and try to sleep.' Paracetamol? So much for sympathy.

The next day was better and within a few weeks I was completely healed. I won't be getting any more tattoos, but I love the one I have. It's a small red apple with a green leaf: my private badge of recovery from ten years of anorexia; a memento of my first book and a reminder that no one can live on an apple a day. It's also a prompt to sometimes make decisions on a whim, to do things that make me happy; a pledge to myself to keep on letting go.

Chapter Eight

STOP, DROP AND YOGA

My boyfriend walks in the front door, talking to his brother who he has just picked up from the airport. I'm standing on my head in the living room, so I give them an upside down smile. They stand in the hallway, staring at me, bags still in their hands. I suppose this is a strange way for me to meet T's brother for the first time.

When I signed up for the Transformational Retreat in France, I'd been drawn by the scientific claims of neurofeedback, but felt very wary of the mind-body-spirit aspect. I'm really not into New Age stuff, and didn't have a spiritual bone in my body. I thought the regular massage sounded great, but I had no idea what 'bodywork' was. As for the yoga, I was downright sceptical.

Numerous friends, as well as doctors, had recommended yoga to me over the years, for its mind-calming benefits, for insomnia, for migraine. Yoga is an ancient art based on a harmonising system of development for the body, mind and spirit. The word 'yoga' comes from the Sanskrit root, *yuj*, which means 'to join' or 'to yoke'. I had tried various forms, from ashtanga and Iyengar to hatha, but I didn't find it physically rigorous enough, and I could never switch off my racing thoughts. I had always felt irritated by the virtuous Bikram bunnies in my office, trotting off to classes at lunchtime with their colourful mats tucked under their arms.

Yoga infuriated me because it requires mental as well as physical discipline. I felt I was deficient in some way: missing the nirvana gene, or that special something which would enable me to reach inner peace. I was good at running, cycling and swimming, but bad at anything that required me to slow down. I didn't immediately 'get' yoga, so I dismissed it.

I had also dismissed meditation and mindfulness. I believed those mantras: 'If it isn't hurting it isn't working' and 'No pain, no gain'. What was the point of sitting motionless with my eyes closed when I could be outside working up a sweat? Being gentle or kind to myself, developing peace of mind, proved impossible. Either I felt guilty, or bored, or restless. So I rejected this mind-body-spirit stuff, instead relying on a hardcore spinning session or a 10 km run to blitz my anxiety.

I've come a long way since then: now I simply can't imagine my life *without* yoga. My conversion took place on that Transformational Retreat.

The alarm went off each morning at 5 a.m. In the chilly darkness of my attic bedroom I dressed in yoga pants and vest, brushed my teeth and splashed cold water on my face. I crept barefoot down the creaking staircase of the manor house and across the yard to the barn, pushing open the heavy wooden door. Upstairs Kate would be sitting at the front of the studio in the lotus position. The barn smelled of incense, with tea lights flickering in the recesses of the stone wall, sky-blue mats laid out on the bare floorboards, a tartan rug folded at the end of each. The huge casement windows were left open to the forest beyond, the breeze and the whispering leaves.

No one was more surprised than I was to find myself utterly hooked on those early morning sessions. Afterwards, standing in the shower, dressing to join the others for breakfast, my mind felt clear and alert. It was incredible to find that I'm not so unspiritual after all; to find real joy and serenity in the practice of yoga.

It is also, contrary to my previous beliefs, very good exercise. Yoga strengthens the muscles and bones, improves flexibility and balance, and benefits the joints, spine and all-round posture. It lowers blood pressure and blood sugar, and reduces the risk of diabetes, heart disease and stroke. It strengthens the immune system, lymphatic drainage and blood flow around the body. The more relaxing yoga poses are restorative too, reducing stress and cortisol, promoting clarity of thought, improving sleeping patterns and boosting mood, happiness and self-esteem.

Many of these benefits overlap – which isn't surprising, given the intimate connection between physical and mental states of health. Think about it: do you stand taller when you're anxious or when you're feeling confident? Do you feel more attractive when you're depressed or when you're happy? Do you sleep better when you're stressed or when you're relaxed? Do you get that recurrent complaint – whether it's migraine, IBS, eczema or whatever – when you're run down or when you're rested?

The benefits of yoga seem to reach into every corner of my body. On the path to letting go, it has been invaluable.

As young children we master new skills constantly – learning to crawl, walk or talk, for example – but as we approach adulthood that process tails off. We declare that we're either good or rubbish at something: 'I'm hopeless at languages', 'I can't draw' or 'I'm the world's worst public speaker'. Once we have decided, or been told, that we're not sporty or sociable or artistic, we rule out entire areas of development.

Most of us love making new friends, listening to new music and tasting new food – but when was the last time you learned to *do* something new? I know it had been a long time for me… Which explains why I'm proud of my headstand!

'By doing an unassisted headstand you've actually managed to turn your world upside down, to see things from a new perspective, to do it without help and to feel happy about it! Inversions are very powerful for hormonal balance: they are your body's inner pharmacy. Plus you are elevating your heart above your head, both literally and at a mind/body level.'

An email from my yoga teacher, Kate. Six weeks earlier, at the Transformational Retreat in France, I had watched in astonishment as Kate demonstrated a headstand – or *shirshasana* – supporting herself only on her forearms and head. When she asked the class to give it a try ourselves, we laughed. Kate and another student helped me into an upside-down position against the wall, but as soon as they let go of my legs I toppled gently on to the mat. 'There's no way I can do that,' I said. 'I simply don't have the upper-body strength.'

Now I'm happily standing on my head for a few minutes every morning and evening, unsupported and steady. I really miss my headstands if I forget to do them. The inversion balances me – as Kate's email explained – and it clears my head in the morning and before bed. It's also a good opportunity to meditate: there's not a lot else you can do while upside down except focus on your breathing.

That's the other reason I'm proud of my headstand: it represents a major change of attitude. By developing yoga practice, I'm working on my spiritual well-being, rather than just choosing the hardest exercise around. I'm letting go of the constant drive for self-punishment. Yoga gave me a sense of peace which has eluded me since childhood, and brought me back into my body.

Yoga has always been cool, but in recent years it has reached cult status, with new forms springing up worldwide. Every ability and taste is catered for: from pregnancy yoga to equine yoga, cannabis yoga, aerial yoga, naked yoga, laughter yoga – even tantrum yoga. In the summer of 2014, the Shard in London launched a programme of yoga sessions 1,016 feet above ground level, and a rash of rooftop classes followed suit across the city, offering high-altitude yoga with panoramic views.

The retail side is booming too, with Lululemon to Sweaty Betty to Bodyism now significant brands in the female clothing market. Forget the days of baggy tracksuit bottoms and old T-shirts; these days 'activewear' is aspirational and beautiful. Top designers such as Calvin Klein and Alexander Wang have their own fitness lines, with everything from sports bras to leggings, to zip-up hoodies and sweatpants. The traditional sports brands have also upped their game, with luminaries such as Stella McCartney designing for Adidas' yoga range. In 2014, the high-end fashion website Net-a-Porter launched a spin-off, Net-a-Sporter, to cater for the growing fashion-fitness demand.

And it's chic to wear your workout gear everywhere, as demonstrated by our beloved female celebrities: popping to the supermarket, on the school run, walking your dog on the beach (if only I lived near a beach). Fitness chic sends a message to others that you're living a healthy lifestyle 24/7. With your capri leggings, crop top, sunglasses and bottle of water, you've either just been for a workout or you're on your way there. Oh the dedication.

I should say that I could happily spend the rest of my life in yoga pants. They're incredibly comfortable, and far more flattering to the average female figure than boring old leggings, cycling shorts, or any combination of leotard and legwarmers!

Yoga is massive on social media. Instagram, Pinterest and Twitter are heaving with accounts from @yogadork to @ FatBuddhaYoga to @DailyCupofYoga. Thousands tweet their ambitious poses, with hashtags such as #stopdropandyoga, #yogaeverydamnday and #inversionjunkie. (If I ever start tweeting selfies of my *shirshasana*, please confiscate my phone.) All over the Internet yoginis compete for the ultimate body bendiness, Instagramming their cobra pose or their exquisite standing bow. They perform handstands on skyscrapers, backbends on beaches, they sit in the perfect lotus position beside the perfect sunset. And yoga is no longer a solitary pursuit: you can do it with your dog (doga), with your partner – relationship selfies of couples in intimate yoga poses – and some 'yoga moms' even do it with their baby.

Speaking of 'yoga moms', Gisele Bündchen is one of many models who has tweeted herself practising yoga shortly after giving birth, looking enviably svelte and stream-lined. Forget leaky boobs, sleepless nights or caesarean scars: for supermodel mothers like Gisele, Miranda Kerr and Alessandra Ambrosio, postpartum yoga looks blissful. I doubt if executing a perfect sequence of *asanas* in immaculate yoga gear while kissing their newborn is a state that many 'normal' new mothers can attain. Of course for supermodels and celebrities, their image is an extension of their brand, so it makes sense that they broadcast every aspect of their flawless lifestyle and life. For the rest of us, yoga could be the ideal opportunity to let go of self-criticism, body-anxiety and the pressure to be perfect.

It seems strange that yoga, with its fundamentally non-materialistic Eastern roots, has become such a fertile ground for self-promotion. The preoccupation with the sleekest yoga outfit and the hottest yoga body is quite a recent phenomenon. Much of the social media dedicated to yoga focuses on extreme elements, often with an emphasis on obsession, power and pain. Pain, power and 'competitive yoga' are fundamentally at odds with the ancient practice and philosophy. Yoga isn't about beating anyone else or setting a new world record – it has never been part of the Olympic movement. As my teacher reminds me, when I bemoan my wobbly standing bow, 'that's why it's called a practice'.

Now, I don't think about being good at yoga – just about the activity in and of itself. When I step on to the mat, I focus on being in the moment, breathing deeply, the sensation of stretch or stillness in my body. At times, yoga will involve intense physical effort; at other times it may just be lying in child's pose (*balasana*) in a profoundly relaxed state. What could be less competitive than that? Whatever the personal challenges we face, I believe yoga helps: boosting our resilience, calming our doubts, building patience and inner calm. Where I used to be hooked on constant movement, burning energy, running harder and faster, consuming less, driving myself into the ground – yoga helps me slow down. In letting go of the past, I've let go of the compulsion to do *more more more* on *less less less*.

At its heart, Buddhism is about overcoming selfishness and self-centredness. The Buddhist term *sangha* translates as 'community'; it teaches that it is only by dispensing with self and ego that one can attain liberation. Next time you're gazing enviously at that supermodel's perfect *pincha*, or about to selfie your magnificent mountain pose (*tadasana*), remind yourself that pouting for the camera has no place in yoga. Remember, 'The flower does not compare itself to the flower next to it. It just blooms.'

As well as opening my eyes to the power of yoga, the French retreat also introduced me to meditation. At the end of each dawn session, and again in the evening, we'd sit on the mats, eyes closed, tartan rugs around our shoulders against the chilly forest breeze. Kate would take us through guided relaxation exercises.

My first attempt at meditation was hopeless, of course: my mind wandered, I got restless, I had an itch I needed to scratch, I shifted about, I felt bored. Day by day, it got easier. I came to see that my discomfort was part of the process: I had to experience the frustration of sitting still before I could discover the joy that sitting still can bring. Once I stopped trying consciously to empty my mind, once I accepted that there was no right or wrong method, I began to look forward to meditation. The combination of rhythmic breathing and simple visualisation was hypnotic. Often when Kate chimed her Tibetan bell at the end of 15 minutes, I found myself in a near-transcendental state.

Meditation is quite the twenty-first-century thing. The Huffington Post has described it as 'the habit of outrageously successful people', citing Rupert Murdoch, Oprah Winfrey and Arianna Huffington among its adherents. Huffington lists early morning yoga and meditation as two of her 'joy triggers', and her company the Huffington Post offers classes to employees.

When the Murdochs and Huffingtons are on board, there's no doubt that meditation has gone well and truly mainstream. Those media moguls are hardly the greatest role models if we're looking for genuine inner peace – but they're clearly on to something. One of the most popular apps of recent years is Headspace, which markets itself as 'gym membership for the mind'. Its creator Andy Puddicombe is a former Buddhist monk and has been hailed as the 'Jamie Oliver of mindfulness, spearheading the meditation movement'.

There is good empirical evidence that meditation can help with stress, anxiety, poor concentration, relationship troubles and addiction, among other modern problems. Mindfulness is similar: researcher and author Jon Kabat-Zinn defines it as 'paying attention in a particular way: on purpose, in the present moment and non-judgmentally'.

When was the last time you did absolutely nothing? Not lying down to sleep – just sitting or lying down, in the middle of the day, with no book, tablet, TV, music, eyes closed. Try it for ten or 15 minutes. When there are truly no distractions, you begin to grapple with your own thoughts. It's harder than it sounds.

Yoga and meditation are challenging for precisely this reason: they give you nowhere to hide. When you're running around the park, working out in the gym, or playing tennis, there's always something to distract you – traffic, loud music, other people. Most physical activity, while mentally therapeutic, doesn't force you to come face-to-face with yourself.

It's only since the retreat that I began to notice how disjointed my attention was; how hard I worked to surround myself with distractions. At home the radio was always on, the Blackberry was flashing with emails and texts, I was never without interruptions. I rarely focused on just one activity: like most women, I was constantly multitasking; doing squats and lunges while brushing my teeth, listening to a podcast while I tackled the ironing. If all else failed, there was always something happening on Twitter. Absolute quiet was rare. Adjusting to silence was hard.

So meditation was even more of a challenge for me than yoga. The moment I stop being active, sit quietly and try to clear my mind, all sorts of irrelevant, unwanted, random thoughts rush in. If you've ever tried simply to focus on your breathing and nothing else, just for a few minutes, you'll know what I mean. I still get frustrated at not being able to attain the ultimate karmic equilibrium: why am I thinking about what to buy for dinner when I should be far away in some kind of Zen bliss?

If like me, you worry about your imperfect meditative technique, remember that there is no right or wrong way to do this. Experienced meditators are able to sit motionless in the perfect lotus position for hours, of course, but it doesn't matter if you can't. In fact, it should never become 'easy' or routine – at all levels, we should strive to keep the enthusiasm of the beginner.

Like yoga, meditation is often adopted as a 'lifestyle' hobby, a glamorous pursuit involving bindis and henna, silk robes and flashes of enlightenment. Far from being a private practice, it becomes something to be seen to do, so others can marvel at how deep you are. This is humorously captured in a postcard I once saw, a bearded Westerner sitting cross-legged in Tibet, Thailand or somewhere oriental, with the caption: 'Man, I look spiritual up here on this mountain. I wish someone was here to see me.'

The truth is, without anyone to admire your efforts, meditation can be boring. In those first few sessions I wondered how I'd get through the long minutes of inactivity and total silence. My own repetitive thoughts threatened to bore me to death. I thought I was so in control of my life, so disciplined, and I couldn't even control my own mind.

Meditation is humbling. It takes courage to wrestle with your own inadequacy and inattention. On his 'Web of Enlightenment' blog, the spiritualist writer Benjamin Riggs has a beautiful explanation of why the process is challenging:

This courage to be in space is the basic principle of meditation practice. If you sit until you want to get up, but just continue to sit and watch the desire to get up without being moved one way or the other, you will soon be initiated into this dark space and develop a profound appreciation for the haunting silence of your radiant mind.

And that's the point. It takes patience to keep sitting there, but it is essential. While you're worrying about not being able to let go, you can't let go. We have to let go of that anxiety. Thoughts will come and thoughts will go: the key is to observe them but not get caught up in them. My yoga teacher likens those unwanted thoughts to a lively puppy: if you give it too much attention, it will keep jumping up and wanting more. Just push those thoughts away, gently but firmly. Each time they arise, just push them away.

In his blockbuster bible of mindfulness *The Power of Now*, Eckhart Tolle describes this process as 'watching the thinker'. Central to his argument is the understanding that we are *not* our thoughts, and we are *not* the thinker. Once we realise this, Tolle believes, we're free, and can discover a vast realm of thoughts and emotions beyond the mind.

For those of us schooled in modern psychology, this seems like heresy. It's hard enough to separate who we are from our corporeal selves, let alone to 'disidentify' from our brain. If we're not our minds, and we're not in our minds, who and where do we exist? It's a confusing, even unsettling, concept. Tolle seems to suggest that we're somewhere else, above both our bodies and our brains. Our minds are not intrinsically who we are, they're just voices and thoughts in our heads.

The essential thing is not to get too heavy about it all. Like my yoga teacher, pushing away those puppy thoughts, Tolle reminds us to keep it light: 'One day you may catch yourself smiling at the voice in your head, as you would smile at the antics of a child.'

In other words, we can observe the commentary in our heads, but from a detached – almost bemused – distance. We don't take the content of our minds too seriously, because it doesn't define who we really are. Just as I began to understand about letting go by watching the river flow, rather than trying to hold it back, meditation teaches me that it's unnecessary to try to control my own thoughts. Tolle is right. When we observe, rather than engage with or struggle against, the voices in our head, we free ourselves.

In my own life, when I experience unhappiness, it's usually caused not by the situation itself, but by my own thoughts or analysis of the situation. Feeling angry or hurt or misunderstood, these are simply feelings. They are not reality. The situation itself is what it is, nothing more; it is neutral. Learning not to take the content of your mind all that seriously is immensely liberating.

Meditation isn't the only way to bring peace into our lives. We also need to disconnect, to bring more peace into our daily existence. In our hyper-competitive, super-stressful world, it can seem old-fashioned, even weak, to admit the importance of routine, regular meals, early nights. I know, to my cost, how a distracted start to the day can lead to a distracted and unproductive day. Before I went on retreat, I used to use my Blackberry as an alarm – which meant that when the alarm went off, I'd start checking emails and fiddling around online. I was caught up in the virtual world before I'd even got out of bed.

Even having the phone beside my bed was a stupid idea. I checked my phone several times during the night. When I couldn't sleep I'd start catching up on messages, thinking and worrying about work. No wonder I had insomnia.

Remember that saying, beloved of the Thatcherite four-hours-sleep-a-night generation, 'You snooze, you lose'? If we're on the go non-stop, we must be ahead of the game; frenetic activity, phones ringing and texts pinging and 20-hour working days means we're successful – right?

Wrong. Noise, panic and stress leads to reactive decision-making and bad judgements. The less frenzied the start to the day, the more focused the rest of the day. Quiet routine is increasingly hard to come by, but we need to learn to take time out, to switch off electronic devices, to disconnect from the virtual world and reconnect with family, to walk in nature, or simply to be alone. In a modern sign of the times, tour companies have started to offer digital-free breaks where the location has no Wi-Fi, or where you actually hand over your devices for the duration of the holiday.

Since I went on retreat, I've started having regular 'unplugged' weekends, with no email or Internet – and I always feel better for it. I've also been greatly influenced by something called the Sabbath Manifesto. Founded by a Jewish community group, the manifesto encourages people to slow down their lives, and disconnect from all forms of media and technologies.

Based on the traditional seventh day of rest, the ten core principles are as follows:

1 Avoid technology

2 Connect with loved ones

3 Nurture your health

4 Get outside

5 Avoid commerce

6 Light candles

7 Drink wine

8 Eat bread

9 Find silence

10 Give back

The popularity of movements such as this highlights our intense desire to get back to a more natural way of being: in touch with our physical surroundings and our loved ones. Like *The Primal Blueprint* (see Chapter 5) we crave a slower, simpler pace. We want to live more mindfully.

For me, meditation is simply the best moment of my day. Even when I'm in a rush, or not in the mood, I force myself to sit still for those precious ten minutes every morning. I light a candle and some Nag Champa incense, close my eyes and focus on my breathing. You don't need any training or equipment for this: just your body and a quiet corner. Just as you plug in your phone, your electric toothbrush, anything which needs charging: sit, breathe and recharge your own batteries.

Why have meditation, yoga and mindfulness struck a chord with so many of us? Personally, I've discovered something on the yoga mat that I haven't found anywhere else, not in the packets of Prozac nor the years of therapy, not even in acupuncture or running around the park.

I remember my friend Tamsin telling me that during a horrible divorce, she would lie down on the floor and cry. She would allocate ten minutes of the day, after the children had gone to school, consciously to let go. The important thing was not the crying, but the lying on the floor. I do it often now. Simply lying on the floor – with or without a mat – is incredibly consoling. If you're stressed it grounds you, if you're anxious it calms you, if you're depressed it changes your perspective.

In the opening chapter I extolled the wonders of neurofeedback: for me it was a mind-changing experience. However, the benefits have not been conclusively, objectively, 100 per cent proven – some scientists argue that it has no effect whatsoever. Even if you believe in it, as I do, you have to rely on the practitioners, their intricate scans and brainwave analysis, to prove it has made a difference.

Yoga and meditation, on the other hand, can't be measured – and I don't need to *see* the proof. The proof is my calmer thinking and my happier mind.

We are all, to a greater or lesser extent, frazzled by modern life in the West. Depression is on the increase, loneliness is on the increase; many of us feel materially richer and spiritually poorer. Unsurprising then that yoga, meditation and mindfulness have become more popular as we've become more connected, more exhausted, more stressed. The ancient rituals of body and breath resonate with something that is already within us. Deep down, we know that mindfulness matters, sleep matters, silence matters.

Consciously making time for meditation, for mindfulness, or simply for sitting in silence, can be uncomfortable, but it's crucial. It forces us to slow down and reflect. It enables us to reboot our systems and reconnect with ourselves. Letting go of the 'busy-busy' mindset, the constant digital distractions and the mental chatter, allows us to go out into the world again with calm, clarity and confidence.

Deliberately disconnecting, whether on a daily or a weekly basis, can be truly transformative. To me, it seems miraculous that something so simple can have such a profound effect. Why not give it a try? Let go of the outside world once in a while: unplug, unwind and find a whole new world within.

Chapter Nine

TICK-TOCK, TICK-TOCK: WOMEN, AGE AND FERTILITY

For something that feels so intensely private, the business of women and their wombs is surprisingly public. These days it's rare to open a newspaper or magazine without encountering an opinion piece or scare story about female fertility. Any profile of a well-known woman will invariably dwell on her reproductive triumphs or tragedies: whether she has babies, or may be planning to have them – and if not, why not. The media in general loves nothing more than a miracle pregnancy, a tragic miscarriage, or the latest dire warnings about 'leaving it too late'.

Here's an exchange between Jennifer Aniston and the feminist author and activist Gloria Steinem, during a Q&A session at the MAKERS Conference for female empowerment, which took place in California in February 2014.

Aniston said to 80-year-old Steinem: 'The public has a great interest in our personal lives. I know you've come up against this and I certainly have too – where being a woman and our value and our worth is basically associated with our marital status or whether or not we have procreated.'

'Well, I guess we're in deep s**t,' Steinem replied.

'That's what I thought,' laughed Aniston. 'Just wanted to make sure that was the case. That we are, in fact, in deep s**t.'

Aniston and Steinem are right, of course. Any thirtysomething female who hasn't had children is obviously in deep s**t. Having ruthlessly ignored the health warnings and shagged our way through an endless stream of partners, when we finally eat humble pie and decide we would, after all, like a baby, is it any wonder that our decrepit and much-depleted wombs are unable to bear fruit? If only we'd procreated at our most fertile, in our late teens or early 20s; if only we hadn't banked on IVF, assumed that reproductive science would be there to bail us out; if only we hadn't been so ambitious, so frivolous, so damn choosy. There is even a special label to describe barren basket cases like us: 'nulliparous' women!

Maybe you're single or undecided, or just really busy; maybe you had an early menopause, or you're infertile, or gay, or maybe your male partner is infertile. You may even be healthy, heterosexual and married, and it simply hasn't happened yet. Not having children is not always a conscious choice: often it's just circumstance and time. One day you're in your 20s, focusing on your career, on meeting a life-partner, saving up to buy a home, the next you're approaching 35 and everyone's muttering about biological clocks and time running out.

Nowhere is this question more urgent than in a woman's 30s. No matter how certain (or uncertain) you may personally feel, suddenly it becomes a matter for public discussion. Suddenly everyone – friends, family, the media, your GP – starts to worry about whether you're going to get on with fulfilling your reproductive destiny.

Having lunch with a former colleague recently, this very topic arose. J is 48, she lives with her long-term partner, but they haven't married or had children. I didn't know whether that was her choice: before this conversation we'd never spoken about it.

J said: 'What really annoys me is the way people talk about women *deciding* to have or not to have children. OK, some women get married and stop using contraception and fall pregnant at the perfect time with the perfect man. But for many of us, it's not that straightforward. You can want children in principle but not have anyone to have them with. Or be with the right partner but not be able to conceive. Or – like me – be with a man who, a few years into your relationship, decides that he's not the marrying kind. And he doesn't want children either. So you spend your 30s and 40s thinking: *Should I leave? Should I try to find someone else? Do I want to be a mother more than I want to be with him?*' From her tone of voice, it's clearly been a difficult few decades.

From Helena Morrissey, the CEO of Newton Investment Management, who has nine children, to Deborah Meaden, the millionaire entrepreneur and star of the BBC's *Dragons' Den*, who has no children, the fertility status of high-profile women is an enduring source of fascination. Even for those who are not in the public eye, it's a topic that recurs in virtually every social or professional context. Women who *do* have children are asked: 'How do you juggle motherhood and work?' – the implication being that either their children or their work must be suffering – and women who *don't* have children are assumed to have put their careers first.

Why do we interrogate powerful women about their 'work-life balance' when powerful men never get asked that question? Why do we obsess over the childlessness of talented, successful women such as Kylie Minogue, Cameron Diaz, Helen Mirren or Angela Merkel: from pop music to politics, why is it even an issue? In David Cameron's summer 2014 cabinet reshuffle, several female MPs were promoted to top government posts. The media's first job was to analyse and scrutinise the body shape and style credentials of the so-called 'Cameron cuties'; next they focused on their biological and marital status. The Conservative employment minister Esther McVey ('single, aged 46') was photographed walking up Downing Street wearing a dress with a slit, which was judged to reveal a thrilling amount of upper leg.

Once the excitement over her thigh-flashing dress had subsided, McVey was called upon to justify her childlessness. How dare she be 46 years old, not married and not a mother? In an interview shortly after the reshuffle she told *Grazia* magazine that, although she loved children, she had never found anyone she really wanted to have them with: 'I'm happy with my friends, my family, my job. I've had other friends who had such a burning desire to have children, they have this biological ticking clock. I don't know what happened to mine. Nobody ever wound it up.'

The stigma attached to women not marrying, or marrying but keeping their own surname, or being the main breadwinner in a relationship, is gradually decreasing. But remaining childless is one of the enduring female taboos.

What if you don't actually want children? Not like Esther McVey that you never found the right man to have them with, or time ran out, but you've simply never felt maternal. Or not maternal *enough* to do something as momentous as getting pregnant, giving birth, and then looking after a helpless baby, toddler, child for the next decade and beyond. Because no matter how casually we may talk about it, having a child is actually a really big deal. No other decision we make will change our lives quite so completely: it seems irresponsible – even bizarre – that we don't receive any guidance over the choice to become (or not to become) a parent. I don't recall any discussion about this at school, beyond some perfunctory sex education in biology lessons. A friend who teaches PSHE (personal, social, health and economic) education confirms that this topic is still not on the national curriculum: 'We spend more time on careers advice than we do on whether or not to have children.' Is this topic still not considered important enough; do we, in the twenty-first century, assume that girls and young women will just *know*? And what about boys and young men – doesn't it matter whether they feel paternal? Is it any wonder that many of us struggle to work out how we feel?

A recently divorced friend called Lisa writes a blog called 'Because I Can: Flying Solo in My Forties'. She is refreshingly honest about the life choices she has made – in particular, the choice not to have children.

I've always known I didn't want kids, and have regularly 'checked in' with myself to make sure my head was still in agreement with my heart... Then came the weddings-and-babies years of my 30s – the peer pressure was huge. 'It's just what you do,' friends said. The more they said that the more I questioned it.

One by one, my friends had their children. Many of them struggled to conceive and being child-free, they felt able to tell me about their problems... Some friends admitted to me that they didn't realise they'd had a choice about having children, and that they hadn't expected the 'drudgery' of their post-natal lives. But then they threw themselves into it, happily, and had one or two more children. In for a penny, I suppose... My opting out of it was like choosing not to go to university, have a husband, buy a house – like not ticking a box in the tick-box life. But my gut instinct was right and I stuck to it...

Whenever I get the Sidebar of Questions, including the usual, 'but you'd be a great mum!' I always say, 'I'd make a great bus conductor, but I'm not here to do that either.' I just know I'm not here to be a mother...

According to the Office for National Statistics (ONS) the proportion of women who are without children has almost doubled since the 1990s. The latest statistics show that a fifth of women in the UK now reach the age of 45 without having a child, and this figure is expected to continue rising. ONS figures show that pregnancy rates for the over 40s have more than doubled in the past two decades. Later motherhood is a growing trend: the average age for a woman to have her first child in Britain is now 30, and 35 for university graduates. So, if you're in your 30s (or 40s) with a degree but no baby, you're not alone. And yet the medical profession still classes women in their mid-30s as elderly. Perhaps it's no wonder we feel decrepit if we haven't managed to get the baby sorted (along with everything else) by our 30s.

Lisa's blog makes me think about those life-changing choices, and timing, and regret. The decision over children is particularly fraught for women because we're aware that we can't change our minds later. Unlike men, we can't, in our 50s or 60s, decide to give parenthood a go.

I asked other female friends who opted out of motherhood how they reached that decision. C, aged 56, is head of a large primary school. 'I'm childless by choice and have never regretted it. I work with children all day, so I do love them, but it wasn't for me. My husband feels the same – we agreed before we got married that we didn't want children. We have a fantastic relationship and we love the lives we've created.'

H is 30, recently engaged, and also certain that she doesn't want kids. 'My fiancé and I have worked hard at our careers for the past ten years and we're planning to take a year out and go travelling. I respect the fact that for many women, becoming a mother is a dream, but for us, travelling and having fun together is the ultimate adventure. Why should our family of two be any less valid than a family of three or four?'

G is 34, a lesbian and angst-free about children: 'My purpose in life isn't about reproducing, simple as that. It seems like other people have more of a problem with this than me, but I don't care. I enjoy my freedom, I like to be able to holiday when and where I want, to spend the weekends doing what I want, to read a book or go to watch a film. I simply have no interest in kids.'

My friend R, aged 43, is childless too, but for different reasons: 'I didn't *choose* it, but my relationships just haven't resulted in children. I always thought I'd do the conventional thing, meet Mr Right, get married, have a family – but it just didn't work out that way. I'm fine about it actually. I love being an aunt and godmother, so there are lots of little people in my life.'

R's words are a reminder that there can be any number of reasons for childlessness: random circumstance as much as deliberate choice. So what of those of us who haven't made up our minds: women who have interesting jobs and relationships throughout their 20s and 30s, open to the idea of motherhood in principle, but not so sure in practice? You may be familiar with the thought process: 'Yes, husband and children, I'm definitely doing that. Just not right now...' Are they – are we – playing a risky game?

The TV presenter Kirstie Allsopp sparked a media storm in July 2014 when she told the *Daily Telegraph*, 'We should speak honestly and frankly about fertility and the fact that it falls off a cliff when you're 35.' She went on to say that she would tell any daughter of hers not to bother with university. 'Start work straight after school, stay at home, save up your deposit... And then we can find you a nice boyfriend and you can have a baby by the time you're 27.'

Allsopp's reactionary views caused much anger, and triggered the usual debate over female reproductive choices. While I found her general tone a bit creepy – 'we can find you a nice boyfriend' – it was that comment about fertility falling off a cliff that really caught my attention. Once again, those possibly inaccurate and certainly alarming reminders of our dwindling supply of eggs. We encounter warnings about missing the baby boat everywhere, from the tabloids to the GP surgery, and it's hard to separate fact from fiction. All it does is add to the anxiety for every non-mother in her 30s who might like, given time, luck or the right man, to have a child.

Kirstie Allsopp is 43 years old, with two sons aged eight and six. She considers that she almost left procreation too late: 'I only whistled in there by a miracle'. But there are plenty of instances of women conceiving in middle age. Cherie Blair and Halle Berry both had babies after the age of 45, and Mariella Frostrup is another mid-life mother: 'I had my babies at 42 and 43, an age I wouldn't have chosen, but a decision that has resulted in nothing but the purest form of pleasure. I am neither unique, nor a freak of nature.'

The TV presenter Gaby Roslin discovered she was pregnant with her second child at 41. 'I said to my obstetrician: *But I'm so old!* He told me I was talking nonsense and that he had women of 46 on his books... He said it's not an age thing, it's down to how healthy you are.'

If we all followed Kirstie Allsopp's advice we'd hunt down that 'nice boyfriend' and settle down and have babies in our 20s – but what of the things we might not achieve? We may not be adding to world population, but we're making films, writing books, setting up businesses, ruling countries, researching medical breakthroughs, doing *other useful things*. Having babies doesn't prevent women from doing any of this – many mothers are phenomenally prolific and productive – but not having babies doesn't make our childless contributions any less worthwhile.

Lucy Worsley is the curator of Historic Royal Palaces, a respected author and TV historian, and not a mother. In a 2014 interview she told *Psychologies* magazine: 'I would not say that I've never considered having children, but it never appeared attractive to me by comparison to the other things that I was doing. That is my decision and I'm comfortable with it. But what I resent is the fact that if I were a man, just turned 40 as I have, I could say – right, well I've done some things with my career, let's start thinking about this children business – and I would have about 20 years in which to do so.'

I identify with Worsley's obvious irritation: the gender inequality around child-bearing and child-rearing, the so-called motherhood penalty, remains. No matter how damaging it may be to a woman's career, or sanity, we still expect her to stay at home with the baby. Of course many mothers want to be with their newborn in the early months, and that's great – but men could also consider that option. As mentioned in Chapter 3, figures show that fewer than one in 50 UK men (1.4 per cent of new fathers) took advantage of the government's new paternity leave scheme (introduced in 2014 to offer fathers up to 26 weeks' paid leave, exchangeable with the mother).

And as Lucy Worsley points out, men have far more time – probably decades more – to ponder the procreation issue. The debate around what age women 'should' have children is frustrating on a number of counts. First, life isn't that simple. Having a child is not like deciding to go to university, or deciding to buy a house. What if your partner doesn't want children? What if you're not in a relationship? Second, it fails to take into account the biological factors: some women try and fail to conceive for many years – getting pregnant is a matter of chance. Third, why is such a deeply private choice involving a woman's body and her emotions, a matter for public debate? When was the last time you ever heard anyone discuss what age men 'should' have children?

However frustrating it feels – and I'm aware I get 'strident' on this issue – it's not anyone's fault that female fertility is time-limited. It's a biological fact and as women we need to understand this. But with so many conflicting messages out there, from those cliff-edge-after-35 warnings, to the anecdotal evidence of women having babies well into their 40s, what's the real truth about female fertility?

The facts are in fact less alarming than is widely reported. Yes, women lose 90 per cent of their eggs by the age of 30 (terrifying) but that still leaves them with around 10,000 eggs. Only one egg is needed to make a baby. The majority of statistics quoted on female fertility come not from modern scientific studies, but from French birth records, covering peasant women from 1670 to 1830 – when health, nutrition and life expectancy were radically inferior to modern standards. By contrast, contemporary research is far more hopeful: a 2004 study of 770 European women found that 82 per cent of 35 to 39 year olds would conceive within a year if they had sex once a week. The figure for 24 to 34 year olds is around 86 per cent.

Then again, what's in a number? These random percentages can be misleading. As my GP said: 'Generalising about *all women* in their 30s or 40s is unhelpful. To calculate the likelihood of conception with any accuracy, one needs to factor in biological age, menstrual cycle, ovarian reserve, general health and nutrition, as well as the male partner's age and the quality of his sperm. Every single case is different.' One thing's for sure: anxiety is unproductive. Whatever you decide about babies, it's really no one's business but your own.

It's hard to disentangle the panic around female fertility from society's general distaste for female ageing. Unlike men, women have a clear cut-off point for evolutionary usefulness; after the menopause they are, in a biological sense, redundant (except as grandmothers). It's not only biology: there is a cultural sense that female ageing is shameful. Consider the derogatory terms we use for older women: 'hag', 'crone', 'old bag/bat/biddy/trout', 'cougar', 'mutton dressed as lamb'. Older men are more often described in terms of power, sexual virility, wisdom and experience; their age is seen as a bonus: 'silver fox' or 'old devil'. In general, women become less visible as they age, whereas men become more so; in the commercial industries, a woman's value drastically decreases with age. The actor John Cusack recently commented that Hollywood is 'brutal' for women, observing that many actresses are considered 'menopausal' at the age of 26.

It takes a strong woman to say she loves getting older *and mean it*. One such woman is the actress Cameron Diaz. In *The Body Book*, Diaz extolls the virtues of ageing: 'Who wants to stay young forever? I like being 41. I love it. So much s**t just falls away... Fear, mostly.' She continues: 'It's the best age. That's when a woman knows how to work things, or she doesn't care about that anymore. You just stop being afraid.'

I admire Diaz's positivity, but I'm not sure we all feel it. In a world that places female youth and beauty on a pedestal, the process of getting older is tough. Not only is a woman's worth inextricably bound up with her appearance, but also with her sexuality and her biological capability. Because a man's fertility does not decline quite so sharply, or have the clear cut-off point of the female menopause, the gender–age imbalance endures. Unsurprising then, that we mind more about age: almost without exception, women I know approaching the big 3-0 (or the big 5-0 or 7-0) have expressed more dread than men I know. My best male friend couldn't even remember whether he was about to turn 40, or 41.

Esquire magazine recently ran an article entitled 'In Praise of 42 Year Old Women', by an American journalist Tom Junod. In all seriousness, Junod declares that 42-year-old women are now, officially, 'f**kable'.

> *Let's face it: There used to be something tragic about even the most beautiful 42-year-old woman. With half her life still ahead of her, she was deemed to be at the end of something – namely, everything society valued in her, other than her success as a mother. If she remained sexual, she was either predatory or desperate; if she remained beautiful, what gave her beauty force was the fact of its fading. And if she remained alone... well, then God help her.*

His argument is as loathsome as it is ludicrous: reading his article online, I didn't know whether to punch the screen or burst out laughing. The reaction on Twitter was instantaneous – and merciless:

Katy Vans @katyvans @TomJunod is not f**kable at any age because he is an asshole.

Julie Lawrenz @JulieLawrenz1 The world where @TomJunod lives women are valued by their screwability. Screw you @Esquiremag

Mary Pols @MaryPols That stinking pile of clueless sexism from @TomJunod about women at 42 suggests there must be NO women with any editing power @Esquiremag

It wasn't only women who responded. 'Dear Tom, As a 43-year-old man, I am so glad you wrote this piece. On top of the impertinence of your writing, it shows why no woman of any age will ever f**k you again. And that makes me very happy because the world is a slightly better place now that you can't reproduce again. I hope your sensibilities die with your generation. Sincerely, David.'

The article was absurd enough, even before it was revealed that its author himself was 55 years old.

We're used to seeing rich and powerful older men with far younger beautiful female partners. Take, for example, the lavish Venetian nuptials between the actor George Clooney and the human rights lawyer Amal Alamuddin in September 2014. Clooney's 53 to Alamuddin's 36 makes an age difference of 17 years, but the acres of newsprint covering the wedding barely mentioned this. Can you imagine the media scandal and speculation if the age gap had been reversed? Clooney epitomises that term 'silver fox', and he's considered every bit as sexy in his 50s as he was in his 30s. Why can't we appreciate mature women in the same way?

Despite the long-entrenched gender imbalance, mature women are becoming less invisible. Perhaps it's a consequence of the original supermodels getting older: Naomi Campbell, Kate Moss, Cindy Crawford, Helena Christensen, Linda Evangelista, Christy Turlington – all the 'supers' are now over 40. Perhaps companies are starting to realise that most of their key consumers are middle-aged, affluent and don't want to be patronised with inappropriate advertisements featuring pre-pubescent models. From silvery locks in fashion campaigns, to wrinkles selling beauty products, it seems we may finally be growing up about female ageing.

And women are starting to challenge the status quo. When Bruce Forsyth, in his 80s, recently retired from hosting the BBC's *Strictly Come Dancing*, he was replaced not by another older man, but by a forty-something woman: Claudia Winkleman. It's surprising – and refreshing – to see a primetime TV programme now hosted by two women: Tess Daly and Claudia Winkleman (although we still await the ultimate frontier: a show hosted by a woman in her 80s with a male co-presenter half her age).

The actress Zoe Saldana recently hit back at the ageism in her industry, describing it as 'f**king ridiculous' that she is considered 'expired' at the age of 36. She told the *Sunday Telegraph*'s *Stella* magazine that she was offered the role as a love interest of an actor who was 30 years older than her. 'I said "Eurgh, no f**king way", they said "But Zoe, he's the hottest actor". I don't give a f**k how hot he is, I'm not going to endorse that – not until the day I see more romantic movies with Diane Keaton, Sandra Bullock, Meryl Streep with young hot actors working as their sidekicks. Only then will I say yes.'

Obviously the stakes for female actresses and models are higher than for the rest of us. But for a woman of any age, it's unpleasant to be valued by our youth, appearance and fecundity – to realise that we're in a game of diminishing returns.

I'm not accusing all men of valuing women on their age. Nor am I accusing them all of being commitment phobic – I've had three long-term relationships with men (aged 37, 39 and 41) who were keen to marry and have a family. They weren't looking for women a decade or two younger, and they didn't assume my fertility was about to 'fall off a cliff' as I approached my 30s. But they weren't in any hurry, because they didn't need to be. In their late 30s to early 40s, these men weren't trapped in the same sociobiological pressure cooker as women of the same age. No matter how open-minded – and all three of them were – there's an unspoken awareness that men don't have a sell-by date.

'Thirties. Oh god, *thirties*,' Jennifer Aniston said to *Parade* magazine, when asked what advice she would give her thirty-something self. 'Go to therapy. Clean up all of the s**t. Clean up all of the toxins and the noise. Understand who you are.' Jennifer had a particularly rough time in her 30s: married to Brad Pitt from the age of 30 to 35, before being left for the actress Angelina Jolie, and an unpleasantly public divorce.

Like Aniston says, 'oh god, *30s*'. Every decade has its challenges, and we all face different highs and lows at different stages in our personal lives. When I turned 30, I remember several older female friends telling me that they felt so much more relaxed and confident in their 30s and 40s than in their 20s. Aniston's comments highlight the particular pressure of the fertility clock ticking loudly. For her, the baby-mania has not abated in her 40s: the celebrity magazines maintain a near-constant Aniston womb-watch. But with advances in medical science, this decade of desperation has been, perhaps cruelly, extended into the female 40s. IVF and other forms of assisted conception can be very positive, enabling older and/or infertile women to become mothers. But it can also be negative, offering false hope to many women who do not conceive, despite thousands of pounds and years of heartache.

I'd be lying if I said I didn't worry about fertility. My journey, physically and emotionally, towards motherhood has been strewn with rocks – OK, boulders. Either it has been the right time and the wrong man, or the wrong man and the right time, but I know that no journey is entirely smooth. My first book, *An Apple a Day*, was subtitled: *A Memoir of Love and Recovery from Anorexia*. Love was a critical part of that recovery process; the greatest motivation to overcome anorexia was my (our) desire to have a baby. When the book came out, one of my first interviews was on Radio 5 Live, with the lovely Irish broadcaster Stephen Nolan, late at night.

At the end of the interview, he asked me: 'So that urge to be a mother must be strong; can you describe that for us?' I hesitated. 'What does it feel like?' he said. 'I don't know,' I said.

I remember at that moment I had tears in my eyes. I had to swallow to clear the lump in my throat. 'It's hard to describe. Just, it's a longing – to hold my baby in my arms.'

I heard that interview again recently and I was struck by the raw emotion in my voice. It makes me wonder if I wanted something then that I don't want now. Or if I've given up.

I'd still like to have a baby – and medically I'm fine – but that's as far as it goes. I totally respect and admire women who are brave enough to embark on assisted conception and IVF, but I've decided it's not for me. If it happens, it happens; if not, that's OK too. Maybe recovering from 10 years of serious illness has put things into perspective: I feel gratitude for being healthy, for my friends and family, for my work and the life I've created.

For me, that's enough. The fact is, there isn't a baby-shaped hole... Sure, I have moments of broodiness, but I'm not obsessed with getting pregnant any more. When it comes to baby-mania I've been through the worst of it and I'm out the other side. I've let go of the desperation – and it's a feeling not of resignation but of peace. Whatever happens, I'll be OK.

Perhaps if we let go of the assumptions that all women will automatically feel broody and that all couples want to become parents, then we might be able to accept the cards that life deals us, with equanimity and courage. At present, it's tough for women who *don't* want children, tough for women who *can't* have children – it's even tough for women who *can* and *do* have children. It's tough for men too. Bringing babies into this world is a life-changing experience; deciding not to do so is also an incredibly important decision. Why should anyone feel apologetic, inadequate or selfish for having, not having, or not being able to have children? A child is a gift but it's also a responsibility, and we could all benefit from more respect and information, less judgement and scaremongering. It's time to banish the stereotypes and learn to value everyone no matter what their biological or marital status or age. Only then can we respect others for the life-choices they make, and make our own based on confidence, not panic.

Chapter Ten

LIFE, LOVE AND BREAK-UPS ONLINE

*When an ex unfollows you, it's like
being dumped all over again...*

One of my close friends got dumped three months ago. Within hours her ex-boyfriend had unfollowed her on every social media platform where they had previously been connected, and deleted all photographs of them together. It was as if he were trying to sever all links with her; erasing their past. A few days later she noticed that her ex-boyfriend's Gmail account was still open on her laptop: he'd been checking messages and had forgotten to log out. Nervously at first, and then more brazenly, she began to read his emails. 'I thought he'd see someone else was in his account and log out, but he's rubbish with technology.'

The man in question is actually an idiot – their relationship dragged on for two years, although my friend had often talked about breaking up with him. Now, not only is she dealing with her own hurt pride, she's also reading his offhand comments about her to his friends: 'I never even fancied her' and that their relationship 'fizzled out months ago'. Although she knew it was wrong, in every sense, to keep reading his emails, she felt unable to look away. Even when she saw the sexy messages he was sending to his new girlfriend.

It's not just the character and relationship assassination: being in his email account also gives my friend a really intimate knowledge of his life. She knows that his uncle got diagnosed with cancer, she can check his bank balance, she knows what job interviews he's going for, and what his new girlfriend is into in bed. Imagine, just imagine, someone knowing all this about you. Horrific.

Not logging out of her ex-boyfriend's Gmail account isn't quite as bad as spying, but it's close. I think my friend is in some kind of post-break-up madness: she checks what he's up to every single day! OK, she hasn't actually hacked into his account, but it's an undeniable invasion of privacy. And it's needless, self-inflicted pain. How is she going to get over him if she carries on like this?

I wouldn't have read his emails in the beginning – not because I'm so much more moral than she is, but because I'm a coward. We've all bad-mouthed our exes after a break-up, and I just wouldn't want to know the terrible things he was saying about me. And yet, there's an awful fascination in what she's doing. 'I know everything about his life, all the lies he's telling each new woman,' she says. 'I feel powerful because I see him for what he is.' She may feel powerful, but I'm not so sure... In some ways, his virtual world has become her reality.

It's estimated that we check our phones an average of 150 times a day. A 2014 survey found that a quarter of all men and women spend 'an unhealthy amount of time online', with the figure rising to 37 per cent for those aged 18–25. This age group was most likely to 'display extreme behaviour when using technology', defined as being addicted to social media, 'getting a high' from online shopping, and feeling anxious or distressed when unable to access technology. The other day I left my phone at home and felt distracted – and yes, anxious – all day. Everything seemed oddly slowed down; an important dimension of my life was missing.

Social scientists argue that children and young people are increasingly unable to distinguish between real life and virtual reality. The website ikeepsafe.org reports that 40 per cent of Internet users between the ages of 18–35 regret posting personal information about themselves, and 57 per cent think other people share too much about their personal thoughts and experiences. Even the most avid users of social media, the so-called digital natives (those born during or after the introduction of the Internet) feel that technology is robbing them of their privacy. Harvard scientists have found that our brains respond to self-disclosure the same way they respond to pleasure triggers like food, money or sex. In other words, most of us like sharing online.

But some of us like it too much. There's a fine line between sharing and over-sharing: while tweeting news of your engagement is lovely, filming the actual proposal for YouTube is perhaps excessive. As for couples Instagramming their

#aftersexselfies – this is most definitely TMI. It's not just teenagers who sometimes get it wrong – remember Obama, Cameron and the Danish PM Helle Thorning-Schmidt's 'selfie' at Nelson Mandela's memorial service in 2013?

In August 2013, an American editor Jason Feifer started a gallery of 'Selfies at Serious Places' on Tumblr. It showed young people posing at Pearl Harbour, at Chernobyl, at holocaust memorial sites, outside Anne Frank's house in Amsterdam, even at crematoria and wakes. Photos include comments like: 'Love my hair today. Hate why I'm dressed up #funeral.' Or 'Selfie at the 9/11 memorial #hungover'. Or how about this: 'Selfie from the gas chamber in Auschwitz #selfie #respect'.

Is this inappropriate, insensitive or just teenagers using social media to express big emotions?

A huge chunk of our lives are lived online nowadays: losing your smartphone is a nightmare, potentially giving others access to your bank account, personal messages, cherished photos or videos and all your social media. Sure, we use them to send texts and emails and to make phone calls, but they're also our maps, encyclopedias, diaries, business networks, our entire universe. These little devices have a powerful hold over us.

The digital revolution is changing our personal lives as much as our professional lives. When Tim Berners-Lee invented the World Wide Web in 1989, he didn't invent an instruction booklet: it's still evolving and we're still finding our way. And this is especially true when it comes to friendships, relationships and break-ups.

Communication via social media is both indirect and direct, and there are plenty of ways to get it wrong. Is it acceptable to flirt on Twitter? When do you change your Facebook status from 'single' to 'in a relationship'? Is it ever OK to have a couple photo on your profile? (I would say *no*! Though sadly not everyone agrees with me...) The rules are even foggier when a relationship ends. Choosing to block someone, for example: is this passive-aggressive, or a way of avoiding overt confrontation? Blocking an ex tells them: I'm so over you that I don't want you in my life *at all*. Blocking, unfriending and unfollowing are weirdly public actions, sending a message to the outside world. Celebrity magazines often base their reports of relationship splits on this kind of evidence: 'We can confirm that x is no longer following y', which takes intrusion to a new level.

Ultimately, it's hard – and probably pointless – to have a private existence on Twitter: unless you instigate full-on padlocked account status (which defies the point of using it as a public platform) anyone can read your tweets. They don't need to be logged in or have an account. And yet we continue to scatter our personal details online willy-nilly. I'm not talking about the really serious stuff here – not Edward Snowden, the *Guardian* revelations and the NSA – few of us would kid ourselves that our data is of international importance. We've grown to accept that we reveal information even by sharing on Twitter and liking on Facebook. I don't care if some algorithm can see what I've searched on Google, and I don't mind the NHS using me for their patient statistics. It's our daily, casual communications, email-chat with friends, online purchases, medical appointments, which reveal the most about us, on a personal level – as my dumped friend's experience shows. Frankly, the idea of any ex-boyfriend in my email account is enough to bring me out in a cold sweat. It's the equivalent, in the pre-digital era, of bugging someone's landline, mobile and house, checking their post and reading their diary, all put together.

Nowhere is this truer than with relationships. Some of the most pointless arguments of my life have been caused by technology. You know the sort of thing: a comment that you intended to be light-hearted, which someone misunderstands. Rows can escalate quickly, because they are context-free. It's very easy to send an angry reply without thinking it through – you can't look the person in the eye, or take their hand, or use any of the body language cues that human interaction traditionally relies upon.

If you're already feeling low, instant communication can make you even more unhappy: you've texted them, why haven't they replied? Is there anything worse than seeing your friends' perfect photographs on Facebook, another school-friend announcing how 'thrilled' she is to be pregnant, or engaged or #justmarried. Or watching your followers drop on Twitter, because EVERYONE HATES YOU. In the latest Bridget Jones novel, *Mad About the Boy*, Bridget muses: 'Feel like tweeting disappeared followers saying: Why? Why?'

A friend, who has periodic bouts of depression, told me that going on Facebook makes him feel intensely lonely. 'It's not just the fact that everyone's posting these oh-so-joyful pictures, but for me, the realisation that most of my "friends" aren't real friends at all. There have been times when I've posted "I'm struggling", or "I can't go on like this" – and it's surprising how few people will pick up the phone and check that I'm OK. You get the sympathetic Emoji, of course, but hardly anyone actually bothers to ring, or visit.'

Far from uniting us, digital technology can make us feel even more isolated. The fact that we *can* be contacted, anytime, anywhere, makes loneliness more acute. Nothing is louder than the sound of your phone not ringing.

Worst of all, social media makes getting over relationships harder than it's ever been. We've all heard those miracle Facebook stories, where long-lost lovers are reunited online after years apart – but at the end of a relationship, daily reminders that the other party still exists can be jarring.

Getting over someone can be similar to the process of bereavement, only with different stages. You experience disbelief, rage, hatred, numbness, ambivalence, via crying-jags and revenge-shags, and early-morning flashes of pure despair. But it's hard to forget someone when you can't stop Googling them, or when you're still sending each other tipsy late-night texts; when you can analyse every tweet and update, and scrutinise their photographs... *Is he looking older, more haggard? Why is he smiling, without you? And who is that lurking woman?*

Most of us are familiar with the obsessive over-analysis that accompanies the early stages of a relationship. And it's the same in the death throes, or when the horse is well and truly flogged. Post-split digital interactions are cryptic: is it significant if your ex retweets you? What does it mean if he 'likes' your status update? Who knows what any of these mixed messages mean. As my sister said the other day (of an ex): 'Why the hell is *he* endorsing me for skills and expertise on LinkedIn?'

Pre-Internet, it was possible to cut yourself off: you could throw out their letters, rip up their photographs, hide (or disembowel) the painful cassettes of 'our' songs, or even make a bonfire of the whole sorry mess and dance around it in the garden. Pre-Internet, you might randomly bump into an ex, but the chances were very low. Now you can summon them instantly.

So what are the rules during or after a relationship? From my own experiences – and plenty of mistakes – here are a few ideas:

✳ Keep some things to yourself. Designate areas of your life which are simply private: doctor's appointments or medical diagnoses; intimate moments with your partner; extreme emotions, especially anger or depression.

✳ Check with others: is your partner more private than you are? (Mine is.) You might be happy to share those drunken/romantic/sunset moments with all and sundry, but your partner might feel differently.

✳ What about close friends and family: how much are they comfortable with you sharing? Be especially careful with your kids, others' kids, nephews or nieces: do they really want photos of them on the potty online for evermore?

✳ Keep your smartphone out of the bedroom and bathroom. It just doesn't need to go there.

✳ After a break-up, it's best to cut online contact with your ex.

It sounds ruthless, to 'unfriend' or 'unfollow' an ex, but think about it... Unless the break-up is completely amicable and you're planning to stay in contact, the quicker you start to move on, the better. And get in there first: it's better to be the one unfriending and unfollowing than being unfriended and unfollowed (for your pride, if nothing else).

Whatever the circumstances surrounding a break-up, it's best to take some time away from social media. If you're like me you'll find yourself tweeting meaningful lyrics and lines of poetry: poignant or romantic or vengeful or pointed... Don't do it! Step away from the computer and lick your wounds in private. This is what I mean about the weird mix of direct and indirect on social media: you can send out very private messages in the most public way, but you're likely to end up looking foolish. It will be obvious to others that you're going through a bad patch and it won't resolve matters with your ex. It's definitely helpful to type these tweets or updates or angry emails and send them somewhere, to your mum, sister, an understanding friend or even your drafts folder, but don't put them out in the public domain. Typing and sending or storing them sort of relieves the itch.

If you find yourself covertly checking up on your ex online, going cold turkey is the only way. Do it swiftly, and be ruthless with yourself. Which is more painful, ripping a plaster off in one go, or prolonging the agony? If you're still struggling with the temptation, treat it like a game. How long can you go without checking his/her Twitter? Tell yourself you really don't care what they're up to. Can you do a whole day without snooping? A whole weekend? When you've lasted an entire week, give yourself a reward.

If you're still unable to make the break, there are plenty of tools to help with the job. Although technology is our enemy here, it can also be an ally. Recent helpful apps and add-ons include:

* **Ex-Blocker:** An add-on that removes references to someone from Firefox or Chrome.

* **Mute Tweets:** A Twitter feature that keeps people out of your timeline.

* **Eternal Sunshine:** A Chrome add-on that removes unwanted status updates from your Facebook feed.

✻ **KillSwitch:** An app that searches Facebook deleting all verbal and visual allusions to your ex.

✻ **Ex-lover Blocker:** An app that calls your friends when you try to drunk-dial your ex. If you persist, it ritually humiliates you on your Facebook wall.

None of these will prevent you from walking past his office, or standing outside his house, or playing old songs, or scrolling through former 'happy' photos, or wearing his hoodie to bed, or spraying his aftershave on your wrists in Boots... but you have to start somewhere.

I know how hard it can be. I know the temptation to check online where he is and what he's up to – most importantly, with whom. *Who is that – is it a new girlfriend? Maybe it's just his cousin? Is she pretty? Are they FLIRTING?* It's all too easy to get into a paranoid vortex, investigating some poor unsuspecting woman's life, her age, her work, friends, relationships, going through her Instagram, all because she happens to be standing next to your ex on the ski slope.

This kind of 'research' is guaranteed to hurt: every reference to an ex's life continuing without you is painful. And it's context-free and paranoia-fuelled: how can you know whether she's a colleague, the wife of a friend, a random stranger or a new beau? You go a whole day without checking their timeline, then, like a dieter depriving themselves of chocolate cake, you have a mad-binge-spying session. It's not spying, you tell yourself, just catching up.

I think back to my first heartbreak, when I was 19. He was 3,500 miles away in New York, and the rupture was total: after I left NYC and we broke up, we didn't speak, write or email at all. The situation was entirely hopeless – but still, it took me years to get over him. I wonder how much worse it would have been if I could have stalked him online, tracked his thoughts and activities, seen photographs of him looking happy while I was so desperately sad. The emotional separation – a terrible process when you've been in love with someone – requires distance. Until your lives are properly separate, you can't forget them. And if you can't forget them, how can you begin to heal?

Academic research into cyberpsychology is still in its infancy, but already it backs up what we know, that the Internet can make disengaging from former partners considerably more difficult. Studies from the Massachusetts Institute of Technology have shown that women are particularly vulnerable to the damaging effects of social media, causing us to obsess over past relationships and preventing us from moving on.

A psychology lecturer at Brunel University, Dr Tara C. Marshall, published a paper in 2012 entitled *Facebook Surveillance of Former Romantic Partners: Associations with postbreakup recovery and personal growth*. (She found that those who remain virtual friends with their exes find it much harder to recover: 'After a break-up I found that a large proportion of people are likely to engage in Facebook stalking... And people who do that more frequently are more likely to report greater distress... more negative feelings such as anger, hostility, hatred and jealousy. They also report greater sexual desire for their ex-partner and greater longing.'

Julia Bueno, a London psychotherapist, agrees: 'In the past three to five years, I have noticed a significant increase in clients who complicate the grief of a break-up through maintaining an online relationship with their ex. The temptation to soothe unbearable feelings of loss, hurt and anger by making this contact can be impossible to resist, especially when it can be done at the tap of a finger. I have seen such behaviours become obsessive and, like other addictions, serve to ease distress momentarily, while increasing emotional damage. I encourage cutting off all contact – online and offline – until a client feels more able to think about an ex without pain.'

Stalking, addiction, emotional damage, this is serious stuff. A few years ago I had an ex-boyfriend whose behaviour was quite alarming. I unfollowed him shortly after we broke up, trying to sever ties gently, but feeling horrible for doing so. As soon as I clicked unfollow, I got a barrage of texts saying: 'That's it, I'm leaving Twitter.' He then committed Twittercide, deleting his account, then reinstated it a few days later. He began recording alarming love songs on to SoundCloud and tweeting deeply meaningful lines of poetry. He sent text messages saying: 'Just so you know, I'm no longer checking your tweets.' This carried on for weeks and reminded me how difficult that post-split period can be. I didn't want to hurt him, but his Twitter surveillance was hurting himself. Having been in his position, I completely understood what he was going through.

It's part of the strangeness of Twitter that you never really know who's following you. Anyone can lurk behind their egg profile. As someone who tweets a lot, I have reservations about lurkers. It strikes me as ungenerous – like coming to a party and not bringing a bottle of wine. Why join if you're not going to join in? I'm sure some eggs have good reason for not tweeting: maybe they're shy, or not sure how it works, or genuinely have nothing to say. But some eggs are a bit more sinister. One woman regularly tweets: 'Why do you think that?' and 'Why did you say this?' to any article or opinion I've expressed. Out of interest, I checked her account and the only person she follows is me, and the only tweets (nine) she has ever sent are challenging me.

Having been on the sharp end of anonymous criticism online, I'm obviously biased. But it's easy to fling rocks, or hide behind your pseudonym, while not putting yourself out there. My friend F has a photo of a meerkat as her profile pic. She has never trolled anyone, but she admits that she feels completely at liberty to say what she wants: 'Because no one can see who I am.'

Perhaps it's the lack of accountability that winds me up. It takes a certain courage to express an opinion in the combative arena of the Internet. I remember as a teenager one night at a party playing this stupid game with friends: from a fifth-floor flat, we threw eggs down on to cars below. Peeking out of the window, we could see irate drivers contemplating the sticky mess on their car roofs, but of course they couldn't see us. It was as cowardly as hiding behind an online persona.

To me, furtive tweets and snidey comments are the complete opposite of civilised, grown-up interaction. Pre-Internet, you could write a poison pen letter, but barely anyone would read it, or care. Now, the oxygen of notoriety and publicity is available to anyone, a heady mix of complete freedom and zero accountability or personal risk. Of course I understand the arguments *pro*-anonymity, for whistle-blowers, or for those with embarrassing or private problems. And some users have valid reason for hiding their identities: in China, say, or North Korea, anonymity online is the only way to achieve freedom of speech. But, on balance, I'm anti.

I had a little taste of online abuse in the summer of 2013. Following the publication of my book *The Ministry of Thin*, I had been writing various articles on body image, size and weight. It was an exciting time, with talks at literary festivals, and interviews on TV and radio, discussions which were robust but good-natured. So I couldn't believe that one piece, for the *Guardian* of all papers, could land me in the middle of an Internet storm.

My point was simple. I argued that overweight people and underweight people may have more in common than might first appear. Rather than seeing obesity as a physical condition, as we often see anorexia as a physical condition, I focused on the underlying psychological reasons for over (or under) eating. I wrote that fat and thin people often use food as an emotional tool, rather than as simple fuel. That eating, or starving, becomes a not-very-effective way to numb other feelings or avoid facing our problems. Through my own experiences, I was identifying with others, fat or thin, mentally well or ill, all of us who have lost the ability to eat in a normal way.

But I also dared to say that staying slim, exercising regularly and eating healthily take a lot of discipline – which they do. Moderation is hard work, for every one of us. The old chestnut about being 'naturally slim' usually disguises a very active lifestyle.

A campaign of vitriol ensued, spearheaded by a group of self-proclaimed 'fat activists' in the United States. One woman, who described herself on her profile as a 'f**ked-up, cross-dressing, gender-bending dyke addicted to cheese' said I was forcing her to eat 'apology salad'. I was accused of 'fat shaming' and denounced as a 'skinny bitch'. Ah, the delights of free speech.

Unpleasant as it was, this experience taught me a valuable lesson. It made me see the futility of trying to reason with angry activists in 140 characters, because their rage (or frustration, or sadness) comes from a place within. It proved how impossible it is to have a rational debate about weight these days – I hadn't set out to be controversial but of course those issues always are. It strengthened my belief that one should own up to one's opinions; that only bullies, trolls and cowards stay anonymous. Lastly, it reminded me how little that social media stuff matters, when set against real life, love and family.

Even though we know that social media doesn't *really* matter, it can play a surprisingly dominant role in our lives. Someone who might agree is the writer and social researcher Brené Brown. In 2010 she delivered an inspiring TEDxHouston talk on imperfection and vulnerability, which is one of the top ten most viewed TED talks, and has attracted over six million viewers. She also received a barrage of abuse, which – as is usual for a woman in the public eye – related to her appearance. Brown recalls the spiteful criticism that erupted online, largely focused on her weight: 'How can she talk about worthiness when she clearly needs to lose fifteen pounds.' Another commenter wrote: 'Less research, more Botox.' Yet another: 'If I looked like Brené Brown, I'd embrace imperfection too.'

The tenor of this abuse is particularly ironic, given that Brown's subject matter is courage and human connection.

Weight, shape, age, these are the easiest and commonest targets when attacking women online. Mary Beard, the TV historian and professor of classics at Cambridge, repeatedly comes under attack for her on-screen appearance. She looks nothing like the average TV presenter – in fact she's nearly 60, with long grey hair, natural wrinkles and a fantastic brain! After her appearance on *Question Time* in 2013, an anonymous poster described Beard as 'a vile, spiteful excuse for a woman, who eats too much cabbage and has cheese straws for teeth'. Her features were even superimposed on to an image of female genitalia. Not all the abuse was anonymous: the television critic A. A. Gill wrote that Beard should be 'kept away from the cameras altogether'. Fortunately, she responded robustly, revealing her attackers as the misogynistic louts they are, while also pointing out the sexist ageism that faces women on TV.

Comedian Sarah Millican also responded publicly to the online mauling she received about the dress she wore to the 2013 Bafta awards. In an article for the *Radio Times*, she described her joy at being nominated, the fun of the red-carpet ceremony, and then… 'I went on to Twitter and it was like a pin to my excitable red balloon. Literally thousands of messages from people criticising my appearance. I was fat and ugly as per usual. My dress was destroyed by the masses.' She confessed to crying all the way home in the car.

You may roll your eyes, and think *get over it*, but this stuff hurts. Think of the aspects of your appearance about which you're most sensitive: your weight or shape, your teeth, or your nose – and imagine a group of strangers dissecting them on a message board. Not only are they reinforcing all the physical insecurities you've ever felt, deep down, but they're doing so in public. The criticism is reductive and petty, but it's also humiliating beyond belief.

There is a tendency to believe that anyone in the public eye, any journalist or actor or politician, is bulletproof. As if the moment your name appears in print, or your face appears on screen, you don't have feelings. Brené Brown is a highly acclaimed public speaker, but that didn't make her any less vulnerable. Just like Mary Beard and Sarah Millican, she admits that she cried her eyes out at the time. So what's the impulse behind the abuse? Do Internet bullies have valid reasons for attacking others in public? An article in *Grazia* magazine in 2014 showed the other perspective, from one of these online bullies: 'The minute I sent my first abusive tweet I felt a twinge of shame and regret. But the initial rush became addictive... I know that it's a power trip and it's no coincidence I do it when I'm feeling ugly, insecure or unappreciated.' The self-confessed 'troll' was writing anonymously, of course. Still, her conclusion was honest: 'Trolling is definitely about attention, about getting a wider response from the wider world. Sometimes the Internet can feel like a party you're not invited to, but if you troll, people sit up and take notice.'

The truth is, you don't have to be a TV personality to be vulnerable online. Every time we express an opinion we open ourselves up to criticism or abuse. A narky comment on Facebook, or being red-arrowed on a message-board can feel like a personal attack – on a bad day, even being ignored can hurt! With the prevalence of smartphones, young children are finding that bullying can follow them home from school, even into their bedrooms. Trolls say that their actions get them noticed, but there are better ways to get attention than by doing others down. The odd bitchy comment between friends is normal enough – we all gossip about celebrities – but attacking others, on a personal level, in a public space, is not harmless.

When you find yourself caring too much about the opinion of strangers, or spending too much time comparing yourself to others online, it's time to step back. The virtual world can exacerbate feelings of loneliness or isolation. There have been times over the past few years when it has almost got on top of me! It certainly got in the way of real relationships, real work, real life. The sheer panic, then relief, of disconnecting on that French retreat, made me determined to preserve a corner of my life which is calm, unvirtual, really real. Letting go of the obsession with social media is one of the strongest things we can do.

Despite the problems and risks of using social media, there are plenty of good things to say about new technology. Global communication is fast, news and entertainment are freely accessible, and creativity and entrepreneurship can flourish online. We have almost unlimited information at our fingertips: it's wonderful to be able to search a half-remembered line from a poem, check what a random schoolmate is up to or instantly look up train times. The Internet has also brought people closer around the world, connecting us with strangers we'd never have known otherwise.

It has also brought us Internet dating (a mixed blessing!), online support groups for those with mental or physical illnesses, and fascinating forums for special interest groups and like-minded folk. Then there's the unexpected joy of collective tweeting during major national events – from the London 2012 Olympics to the Eurovision Song Contest, Twitter adds a wonderful dimension. You can be sitting at home watching TV all by yourself in your pyjamas and Twitter makes you feel part of a party. There is a special glow, hard to explain to non-Twitter users, which comes from the random interaction of the Twittersphere. When someone favourites something you've tweeted; when you get into witty banter with a total stranger; when you're flirting, or LOLing, or just complaining about the weather, it can be gloriously unifying. A friend and I email each other when we acquire a famous or even semi-famous follower: she has a well-known TV chef, I have a feminist writer whom I idolise. (OK, my idol follows everyone who follows her – but it's a start!)

As well as Twitter, there's culture and music: I waste many happy hours reading old interviews on the *Paris Review* online, streaming songs on Spotify and YouTube. Just the other day someone sent me a link to W. B. Yeats reading his poetry, recorded in the 1930s. And yes, I'm as guilty of a *Mail Online* afternoon binge as the next person.

Obviously we can't un-invent the Internet. The genie is well and truly out of the bottle; the new digital world is unrecognisable from the world many of us grew up in, only a few decades ago. Before smartphones, before WhatsApp, Snapchat and Tumblr, school was for lessons and friends, and home was for family and homework. Written homework – in a scruffy exercise book with lined pages and a battered old cover – remember that? I tutor a 17-year-old A level student who recently told me she hadn't used a pen and paper 'in, like, months'.

Pre-digital childhood was different, and pre-digital adolescence was even more different. If you were 'seeing' someone, you waited for them to ring you, or you asked permission from your parents to use the telephone. In our house, the single landline phone was in the chilly hallway. When it rang there was always a scramble to answer it – but not too fast, because that was uncool. Then we'd stretch the twisted extension cord as far as possible up the stairs, to get some privacy from the rest of the family. My two sisters and two brothers and I routinely eavesdropped on each other's calls, and then took the mickey out of each other afterwards. Nowadays it's hard to imagine not being able to make a private call from your mobile, or text a boyfriend.

Of course we can't go back to those pre-digital days. I don't even have a landline in my flat – there seems little point – and among most people I know, if they have a fixed phone line, it's for broadband, not for making calls. These days it's arguably more of a hassle to lose your phone than it is to lose your wallet or purse, if you even carry one any more. Think of the multitasking we can do: catching up on news, answering emails, booking train tickets, bidding on eBay, tweeting and liking – it's not uncommon to have six or seven different things going on at one time. There is no doubt we have sped our lives up – but at what cost?

Sometimes it feels like digital chaos. I think we risk losing something precious and uniquely human, the ability to focus and concentrate, to think and feel. With so much happening simultaneously, so much instant gratification and feedback, a constant bombardment of images and opinions and events, our minds are becoming distracted and fragmented. It has affected the way we relate to each other as human beings too: letters, postcards, thank you notes, it all took thought, a postage stamp, a walk to the post-box. We rarely pick up the phone to talk these days, when a text or an email will do. I think we are at risk of taking less care, and caring less, about others.

For all the talk of 'connection' online, we're often connecting with dissatisfaction and FOMO (fear of missing out) rather than connecting with others. Our digital lives are carefully curated; we do our best to portray ourselves as we'd like to be seen, so no wonder other people's online personas can make us feel inadequate. We try to present a 'shiny-happy' exterior: it's a defence mechanism, a way of pretending you're OK. But don't get sucked into the pretence, and don't forget to hug, write and 'like' things for *real*.

Keep moving; keep things fresh. Walk and talk and learn things and go to new places. Don't compare yourself with others. Don't let the Internet keep you trapped in your past, or in your ex's new life. Make sure you're in charge of your own online behaviour, and that it's giving you pleasure and interest, not pain or isolation. Be ruthless: if exes or toxic friends make you feel negative, go cold turkey. Don't obsess over others and envy their perfect life (chances are it's far from perfect). Remember that there is life beyond the screen: getting out into the real world, spending time with real people, and turning off your gadgets will help you let go of the nonsense, insecurity and worry that can plague us in our online lives. When you let go of all this, you're free to start again and to enjoy life.

Chapter Eleven

LOOKING FOR LOVE IN CYBERSPACE

'Some of these profiles are ridiculous! Look at this one – he calls himself Baldrick69.' I hand the phone to my sister...

Are you looking for a short bald ugly man? YES?! Well you my lucky lady have just hit the BLOODY JACKPOT! DING! DING! DING! DING!!! Flashing lights and all that. OK I'm not that bad I'm just below average height when wearing high heels – LOL truthfully I am 5' 5" it's not that bad – I do have a face only a mother could love though. I'm a master-creator of video games and I live in New Cross which is LITERALLY just on the cusp of being cool. Maybe next year. My ideal woman? A head, body, two arms and two legs although I can definitely move on the number of limbs... Breathing would be a plus.

Well, if humour really is the way to a woman's heart, this man was on to a winner. But for some reason, I didn't have the urge to click on 'contact'. My sister found it hilarious, of course, but possibly he was taking things too far.

So why had I launched my boat into the choppy waters of Internet dating? It all started with a break-up, a few years ago. If you've been through this experience yourself, you'll know how rough things get, how stormy your emotions become when your anchor is suddenly swept away. Truly, I was all at sea.

Every morning I'd wake in the early hours, full of regret, sadness, despair. I went over and over the past, analysing where the relationship had gone wrong, whether we could work it out. The future seemed very bleak. Sometimes I didn't think it was possible to feel any worse, and then I'd wake the next day at 4 a.m. and find a fresh source of pain, another wave of bittersweet memories – lo and behold, it could hurt even more.

It wasn't just the break-up I was struggling with; I also struggled with my new single status. I felt as though I were on the scrap heap, unwanted and irrelevant. I knew I didn't need a man to validate me, so why did I feel such a failure without one? The heartbreak got mixed up with the singleness and I was a mess. Some days I felt like I didn't exist.

It was a shock to realise that I was no good at being single. I had always considered myself a strong, independent woman: I own my home, I enjoy travelling solo and going to the cinema alone, I don't need a man to change lightbulbs or deal with spiders for me – and I've known how to wire a plug since

I was about ten years old. From an early age, despite being surrounded by brothers and sisters, I was a very private person. I believed that fulfilment comes from within and didn't depend on others to feel complete.

And yet, the facts told a different story – I hadn't been properly single since my teens. How ridiculous to think of myself as a lone wolf, when there had always been a boyfriend by my side. Why, I wonder, did I maintain this fiction of being independent? Why did I actually need to be in a relationship to feel OK about myself?

Maybe it comes down to wanting to be wanted. The reassurance of being someone's girlfriend, part of a couple. I could 'commit' to a certain extent, but not all the way. I had to be in control in relationships, just as I controlled other areas of my life: notably food and exercise. And I felt profound ambivalence over what I really wanted: in theory, to get married and have a baby, but I was never 100 per cent sure. I recognise types of partner in my past and I recognise patterns of behaviour: me being the one in control, me always leaving (perhaps before I'm left). Maybe my behaviour wasn't so contradictory after all. Maybe this conflict, between being in a relationship and remaining independent, is an impulse that many of us struggle with.

I had tried all the different methods of recovering from heartbreak: wine, self-help books, therapy, exercise. I tried 'embracing my freedom', I tried 'acknowledging the sadness', I tried 'throwing myself into things', I tried allowing myself 'time to heal'. Nothing worked. After four whole weeks of being single, I decided enough was enough. I didn't actually want a replacement for my ex-boyfriend – I was in no way ready, emotionally. But doing something was better than doing nothing: I'd never meet anyone if I sat at home in despair.

So, early one morning while London was sleeping, I got out of bed, made coffee and switched on my laptop. Having Googled various websites, I chose the dating service of a respected broadsheet newspaper. I opted for one with a monthly subscription fee – although there are free sites available – believing that would weed out the timewasters. (You live and learn.)

I entered my credit card details, filled in endless tick-boxes and wrote a brief profile. It was no work of staggering genius: something about being 'lively, open-minded, interested in literature, music and travel'. I had to specify what I hoped for in a partner, in terms of appearance, age, profession, income, geographical location, level of education and so on. In an ideal world I'd have liked to meet someone creative – a writer or playwright perhaps, mid to late 30s, handsome and solvent, living in central London, never married, no children, you know the sort of thing. But I was being 'open-minded' so I kept the parameters broad. Naively, I thought all ages, all areas, all chaps considered (within reason).

I finished my profile, uploaded a recent photograph and went back to bed for a bit more dawn despair. A few hours later I started getting the oddest messages:

Hey-hello,u have a sizzling profile,love how u write,and your phot very attractive, overall u are rather intriiguing,enticed me enough into gettingvin touch saying hi n intruloducing myself,nice to meet you by the way,i am a fun,intrsting n unique guy who knows how to treat a lady RITE, hit me up. Spittin Snake xx

Not the best start.

I'd barely recovered from this enticing proposition before my heart-shaped mailbox flashed again: 'Congratulations! You have a message from Wandsworth Wanderer.' His profile showed an elderly man with long grey hair and a defeated expression. Something about his name conjured up the image of a flasher in a raincoat.

> *Hello. I'm a joiner, 78 years old, living in SW18. I enjoy walking on the Common in all weathers…*

I pressed delete. Even open-mindedness has limits. Over the next few days the messages continued to arrive, each weirder than the next. Why was I getting messages from 78 year olds? Why did Mac from Linlithgow (hundreds of miles away) keep contacting me? I began to adjust my settings: aged 30–50, living within a ten-mile radius of me. There wasn't a tick box for 'pedantic attention to detail' but I specified that I'd prefer some level of higher education. I didn't mean to be judgemental, but I find incorrect spelling and grammar a turn-off. (I once broke up with a man because he held his pen in his fist, like a harpoon. In love letters he would misspell 'you're' as 'your'; imagine: 'your so beautiful'.)

The wrong 'uns continued to write – and I had to admire their tenacity. A man called Doc Martin sent me this after I had ignored his previous seven messages:

> *Well am certainly attracted to you and would like to get to know you if your interested. Im inteligent handsome better-looking in person than*

*in pictures LOL and although I havent read Tolstoi
Im cultured and fun. I love eating out, good wines
which is something we have in common. I love to
travel having seen a lot of the world already but
visiting with some1 new makes it like visiting for
the first time. I love to run and be fit and as a side
effect it does keep me toned if ya know what I
mean! I like the sun but equelly like the rain if I'm
curled up in bed with someone I love in a cottage
listening to it hit the windows and roof. I like to be
warm but I dont mind the cold if its for a reason.
I buy two deserts large plate of cheese after dinner
so there is always enough for two but we can still
share. So what do you think do you fancy meeting
up tomorrow?*

Clearly, the image of the rain falling on a cottage roof was
intended to be poetic. And he wasn't to know that cheese was
not the way to seduce me.

A man calling himself 'Good, Bad and Yummy' made me
laugh out loud with his opening proposition:

*If you're better looking than me, cleverer than me,
funnier than me, and less hairy than me, what are you
waiting for?? Quick, ask me out so we can both get
out of here before someone we know spots us. (I don't
care what anyone says, online dating is embarrassing.)*

I liked the humour and honesty of that one.

There were men who wrote late at night, on the website's instant-messaging service: 'Hey I'm lying in bed... what are you wearing?' I don't think they were looking for a long-term commitment.

I didn't exactly feel the spark with this 39 year old from Rotherhithe either:

> No *illusions that I have any chance to impress girls with my looks/pictures. I'm sort of a misfit, but not crazy. I just see things differently from the rest of the world. I don't fit into the model of 'proper', 'decent' or 'right'. By the way this is not a matter of pride, just an advance warning. At the same time I am a fully grown-up and responsible person. I am looking for a relationship for life. But what does it mean? How would I know? Or any of us?*

I'm not sure if that was a rhetorical flourish, or an existential question. But when someone announces that they're 'a misfit, but not crazy' even before a first date, it's probably time to move along now.

Scrolling through page after page of Internet profiles – some poetic, some arrogant, some rather moving, I began to see how random the process was. How can we convey anything of our individual personality in a few lines, or assess others? How to narrow down potential matches when almost everyone says they're outgoing and sociable, they enjoy travelling, good food and spending time with friends; that they like going out and staying in? And what can you tell about someone from a photograph?

Then there are the endless questions: 'Are you looking for a friendship/casual relationship/no-strings-attached fling/long-term relationship/marriage?' 'Do you want children: yes/no/maybe...' How honest should we be? In all these tick-boxes, the human context is completely absent.

Those romantic stories you hear from older generations, of catching someone's eye on the bus, returning a lost wallet, or just striking up a conversation while walking the dog, those chance encounters have all but disappeared. My parents met at the British Library, when my father held the door open for my mother. They got talking and he invited her to join him for a coffee. The rest, as they say...

These days, everyone in the British Library is plugged into their headphones, furiously jabbing away at their laptops, scrolling on their tablets, swiping and typing – perhaps even looking for love online. I sometimes wonder if we all just put down our gadgets and lifted our heads and looked around, we might begin to see that we're surrounded by possibility.

I found myself increasingly unable to differentiate one profile from another. Exchanging messages helped to establish whether there might be a mutual spark, of course, but really words are just words. It was time to start meeting up in the flesh.

I had subscribed to the website initially for one month – signing up for three or six months seemed too much like commitment – but I was fed up by the end of the first week. Between Spittin Snake, Linlithgow man, and the septuagenarian Wanderer, something seemed to have got lost in translation. The website boasted of its 'perfect-match' compatibility software and high success rate, but I often felt I'd have found a closer match by walking into Trafalgar Square, blindfold and drunk, and randomly grabbing a passer-by.

My friend Karen, who met her husband-to-be online, encouraged me to persevere. My mother said: 'Well, you know what I think about men one meets online.' (Somewhat unhelpful, I felt.) My sisters found most of the profiles hysterically funny. My friend Libby said: 'Don't be too choosy – you never know who could turn out to be Mr Right...'

I honestly wasn't being choosy. Despite all my reservations about online dating, I was determined to keep an open mind. In among the oddballs, there were some hopeful prospects, messages in which there was a genuine rapport. And so it began. Evening after evening I'd muster my energy, blow-dry my hair, put on a bright date-face and make my way to Covent Garden or Chelsea for the requisite awkward first meeting.

Even when I knew I wasn't interested in someone from the moment I met them, I still felt obliged to stay for a few hours, to make an effort. Why, I wonder? Why didn't I just finish my glass of wine and leave – why not say 'I don't think this is going to work' and save us both the time and money of a wasted drink?

The enforced 'going out' quickly became a chore. I was writing and filming by day, and heartbrokenly sleepless by night, and in the evenings I just wanted to hunker down. Meeting a stranger, telling the (abridged) version of your life story, finding out about theirs, is emotionally draining.

Most evenings were a let down. Real life attraction is so different to attraction online. Dating websites categorise the basic facts – height and weight, age and income – but none of this captures the true person. Human connection depends on myriad factors: the way someone moves, their body language, their voice, the way they smile, even the way they smell. It's these indefinable sparks that make human attraction so unpredictable (and it's probably what leads to infidelity and divorce). The men with whom I've fallen in love most deeply have been far from conventionally good-looking and I find vanity the deadliest turn-off. A friend recently called me a 'sapiophile'. Once I looked it up – '*Sapiophile* (noun) means someone who is sexually attracted to intelligent people' – I had to admit she was right.

It can be surprising to discover who and what we find attractive. Many of us talk about having a 'type' but in reality it's just a fiction: you may think you go for brooding, artistic men and end up with a sporty, outgoing chap who prefers rugby to reading. And we often find ourselves falling for people gradually, as we get to know them: friends, colleagues, people we spend time around and grow towards. I've met handsome men who I'm not remotely attracted to; but I've fallen head-over-heels for slightly geeky types, paunch and all. For me, there is no automatic association between good looks and sexual chemistry.

My evening with Mark was a good example of this. It came early in my online dating journey, before I had learned to rein in my expectations. The pre-date interaction had been positive: we had exchanged emails, talked once on the phone, and he sounded sparky, warm and funny. He even lived near me. His profile name was 'Infinite Potential' (which seemed promising, if a little ambitious).

We arranged to meet at The Albion pub. So far so good: Mark was waiting when I arrived, tall, dark and rather handsome. He was expensively dressed – jeans, white shirt, well-cut jacket. It was a warm evening and we sat in the beer garden with an excellent bottle of white wine. And he began to talk. And talk. And talk. Perhaps he was nervous, perhaps I was having a bad day, but his monologue drained me of energy. As he droned on, I pictured him at a party or in a meeting, sucking the oxygen out of the room. There was no interplay of ideas, no conversational give and take, and absolutely zero spark. I regretted the bottle of wine – why hadn't we just got glasses – and cursed my inability to leave. He held forth on his career prospects, his family, his collection of cars, his house. When I crowbarred my way into the monologue, he was perfectly able to listen, but then he went back to his favourite subject: himself.

Over the next few weeks I met many more Marks, or men like him. Disappointment became a familiar emotion, as I came home from yet another so-so date. The men often texted or emailed afterwards, asking to meet again, but I rarely bothered with a second date. Was I being too fussy? They were clean, intelligent, solvent, sane. Nothing was wildly wrong, but something was missing. I felt frustrated with myself, as I've felt frustrated over the years, every time I've ended a perfectly OK relationship. Why not make a go of it with someone pleasant? I'm certainly not perfect – on the contrary, I'm riddled with faults – so what was I holding out for? I suppose I was learning that compatibility isn't as simple as a few tick-boxes on a screen.

I also learned that you should read a profile properly before agreeing to a date. After a pleasant exchange of messages, I met up with Alistair: 43 years old, tall and nice-looking. We talked for an entire afternoon over pots of Earl Grey in Le Pain Quotidien opposite Southwark Cathedral. He was highly intelligent: a Cambridge-educated mathematician, chess master, designer of online poker games and classical singer. He was sharp and witty: unlike Mark, he remembered to ask me about myself. He even suggested a glass of wine in the bar at the top of the Gherkin, which we arranged for later that week.

We were leaving the cafe, still talking and laughing, when Alistair said this: 'I can't stand it when women initiate contact first. I actually get messages from divorced women *in their 40s!* Divorced women in their 40s *with children!* They're clearly just looking for someone to bankroll them...' In a few minutes, he'd flipped from being highly attractive to nasty, ageist, even misogynistic.

I didn't know what to say. I couldn't understand why women *in their 40s* were so repellent to Alistair (aged 43). Nor why women *with children* were such a horrifying prospect. That evening I read his profile properly, and found the clue: 'I'm bookish, cookish, foodie, NOT BROODY.' I sent him a text to cancel our drink, saying I had urgent work commitments in the United States (for the foreseeable future).

In person, until that comment, Alistair had seemed a great match. On screen, Mark had ticked all the boxes. But perhaps there was a reason they were having trouble getting a second date, however harsh that sounds.

This is the catch 22 of plunging back into the dating scene in your 30s. I was starting to think: *No prizes for guessing why he's single.* Or, *By this age, all the good ones are taken.* But it was a self-fulfilling prophecy; if I truly believed that, I might as well have given up then and there.

I found it depressing though, trawling through these websites, looking at us all piled high in the same boat, navigating the waters of our early-mid-life-crises, desperately searching for a life-raft, or someone to cling on to…

But life is full of surprises. Love is unpredictable. When my first month's subscription to that dating website expired, I wanted to throw in the towel. Then I happened to read an interview with a well-known actress who met the love of her life online in her late 40s. She said something that struck a chord: 'I had almost given up when I met him, but you never know who's around the corner. After all, it only takes one.'

I decided to persevere. She was right, you never know who's around the corner – *nil desperandum* and all that! If I was honest, I hadn't been putting enough effort in. I decided to treat the matter more seriously: I'd allocate half an hour every evening to responding to messages and checking profiles. I could even draw up a spreadsheet and treat it like a work project. When I had exhausted all the possibilities of the first website (I kept getting matched to the same profiles, some of whom I'd already been on dates with!) I signed up to a different one.

This is where I encountered Benoît. He was a pocket-sized Parisian, mid-30s, and worked in investment banking. He'd taken an MBA at Harvard so he spoke perfect English, but with a delicious French accent. His office wasn't far from my flat, so we arranged to meet one morning before work, at a busy Starbucks in the city. We drank several espressos, and talked non-stop, and suddenly it was 9 a.m. and we were both running late. For the first time I thought I'd like to see this man again.

I smiled my way through various meetings that morning. When I switched my phone back on there was a text from Benoît, asking if I was free the following night. He proposed 'a drink, or dinner, or a film at the Barbican – or all three'.

There was a re-run of the arthouse film *The Beat That My Heart Skipped (De Battre Mon Coeur s'est Arrêté)* and he booked tickets. We had a glass of wine beforehand, discussing the relative merits of Paris and London, nuclear power versus renewable energy, Tolstoy versus Murakami, and more besides. Just as everything felt wrong, talking to Mark, everything felt right, talking to Benoît.

I can still remember everything about that evening. Leaving the bar, he held open the door, and then gently took my hand. I looked at him and he just smiled. We walked through the post-work crowds along Moorgate, into the Barbican complex and around the labyrinthine corridors to cinema 3. He kept holding my hand throughout the film (but it wasn't sweaty as I remember teenage hand-holding used to be). When the credits rolled we stayed in our seats, listening to the music, just looking at each other. When the auditorium was empty, finally, infinitely slowly, we kissed. Now I understood the title of the film.

I didn't expect to meet someone like Benoît on a dating website. The chemistry between us was intense. Heartbreak saps your confidence and your libido, and I hadn't been feeling sexy for a long while. I had forgotten what it felt like to be so consumed with lust that you can't sleep, eat or think straight. We'd meet for lunch at a gastropub in Belsize Park, near where he lived, then walk on Hampstead Heath, then lose entire afternoons at his flat.

This came at a good time for me. Winter was approaching, and winter is hard when you're depressed or lonely. The passion didn't eradicate the heartbreak, as such, but it reconnected me with my body. Anyone who has experienced the disintegration of their relationship knows how painful it can be. This liaison distracted me from the constant memories. And it was honest and mutual. Frenchmen know how to make women feel wonderful: I was desired and I felt desirable.

But my heart was still fragile. Sometimes when Benoît kissed me, I had to blink back tears. I felt guilty and I felt sad. It was barely two months since my relationship had ended, and I was in no fit state to plunge into something new. Lust is easily confused as love, and I was very confused. Strong emotions threatened to tip me over the edge.

I remember one night at Benoît's. I couldn't sleep, and was sitting in his large open-plan lounge, staring at the embers of the fire we'd lit earlier that evening. I recalled a phrase I'd read, years before, written by the mystic Rumi: 'You have to keep breaking your heart until it opens.' My heart was broken, and full, and empty, all at the same time.

Benoît and I carried on seeing each other throughout the autumn. As Christmas approached, he invited me to join a group of his French banker friends skiing in St Anton. Without much agonising on my part, and I hope without hurting him, it dawned on me that we lived in different worlds. I knew that eventually he planned to move back to Paris. He'd spend the winters in Anton or Verbier, and the summers in St Rémy. He'd marry a chic Parisienne and they'd have two immaculate children. That wasn't me. Much as I loved that season of reawakening with Benoît, I knew it was just that: a brief, magical season. Even now, when I cycle past our first-date Starbucks, I smile.

That short relationship may not have worked out, but it made me happy. And it proved that I'd been wrong about online dating: it wasn't just for losers. In total, I met up with more than 20 different men – some only once, some several times. I'd been rather idealistic when I first subscribed, thinking that if I had arranged one date, I shouldn't arrange any others. This was incorrect, of course: successful dating requires a scattergun approach. I needed to be like one of those Manhattan types, you know the women who schedule their dating diaries ruthlessly: Brad for power breakfast after the gym, lunch with Tyler, cocktails with Channing, dinner with Dylan…

Everyone was different, and memorable in their own way. There was James the laywer, Andrew the property specialist, and Kenny Jr, an editor from New York. James and I disagreed on almost everything, and I think Andrew was gay but in denial (judging from his flirtation with the barman on our sole date). Kenny Jr was a former water-polo champion with an excellent swimmer's body, editor's brains – and an obsession with beating his front crawl 'personal best'.

I met Javier, a hippy in his 40s who taught children with special needs, wrote abstract verse and talked non-stop about the Occupy movement. Christopher, wearing red trousers, took me to the top of the Shard: we sipped champagne and awkwardly pointed out famous London landmarks like tourists (even though we both live in London) because we had nothing else to talk about.

What with online dating, work and friends, I didn't lack for male company. But I was doomed to an endless cycle of disappointing blind dates. Fast running out of enthusiasm (and mascara), I began to ask myself why I was even looking for a man. The more wrong matches I met, the more I realised that I really enjoyed my own company. Gradually I began to confront my discomfort over 'being single'. I wasn't completely over the break-up, but I was doing OK on my own. That desperate early feeling – *I can't imagine life without him* – had receded. For the first time I could think clearly about the future, whatever it might hold; there was less compulsion to replay the past or try to fix things. What I'd needed was not a new man, but some time alone. But it took this seemingly endless sequence of dates for me to find that out.

In retrospect, I was lucky. Five years ago, when I was first trying Internet dating, it had lost the shameful stigma of the early days, but it hadn't yet taken on the casual, almost throwaway quality it now has. Statistics show that around nine million Brits use an online dating service every year, by far the highest levels in Europe. And yet we're also staying single for longer. Experts in cyberpsychology warn that men and women are increasingly dependent on virtual communication, and many have forgotten how to communicate in reality.

A male friend tells me how he uses Tinder. 'When I'm on the train, or bored at work, I'll spend ages checking out girls' photos, right-swiping the ones I fancy, left-swiping the ones I don't, but that's it, I never take it further. In six months of using Tinder I've met up with two girls in the flesh, and they looked nothing like their photos.' When I asked him if he actually wanted to find a girlfriend, he looked doubtful: 'I don't know if I can be bothered any more. There are so many options, so many photos – going on an actual date seems like a lot of work.' A female friend tells me: 'I actually think Tinder is making me more resistant to chatting guys up and putting myself out there. In a bar last weekend I was sitting near a group of good-looking, friendly men. But could I talk to them, or even smile their way? Did any of them offer to buy me a drink? NO – because we were all too busy staring at our screens.'

There's no doubt that having apps like PlentyOfFish, OKCupid or Happn next to our eBay and Asos apps takes the romance out of it. Scrolling through thousands of potential, pouting hot lovers online, we become desensitised to the real, human experience of smiling, approaching, flirting, being rebuffed, all those uncertain, exciting elements of getting to know a real person. It's far easier to accept or reject the profiles of people you might never have to engage with, than risk a real-life encounter. We can send an anonymous message and not deal with the consequences. If it gets awkward, we can just log off, or switch to a bout of Angry Birds instead. Why would we bother with expensive, noisy, stressful nights out with real dates when our smartphones can supply thousands of gorgeous singletons, all waiting to message us at the swipe of a finger…

Perhaps Internet dating is a game of numbers, and you have to kiss a lot of frogs before you find your prince. Perhaps it's random: you might meet 500 frogs and no prince, or your prince might be the first person you meet. Or you might find your prince but not be his princess. There are a lot of frogs hopping around online, that's for sure.

I think learning to be alone is one of the most important life lessons of all. Online or offline, there's no guarantee that any relationship will last. We shouldn't found all our hopes on another person, nor should we fear the solitary state. There is still a stigma to singleness – especially for us old maids, I mean spinsters, I mean women – but it doesn't need to be that way. Being single can be lonely, but so can being in the wrong relationship.

When things get tough, especially after a bad break-up, it's easy to attack oneself. You know the feeling: you've been rejected or abandoned, so you tell yourself you must be to blame. It's at these times, when you feel most like a failure, that you need proper nurture. While you're getting your mojo back (or licking your wounds) do whatever helps – whether it's drinking tea at your mum's, or going clubbing with friends, or staying in alone. If you need to watch a lot of bad reality television, or drink a bottle of wine, or eat a whole box of Godiva chocolates, that's OK too. (Maybe not every night for the wine/chocolate.) Instead of being harsh on yourself, step back and ask: what would I say to a friend who was struggling like this? Would I be judgemental about their situation, or compassionate? Try some kindness towards yourself: you have enough on your plate without adding self-loathing. As well as reminding me of the value of my own company, Internet dating kept me from too much weeping and woe. It didn't always work – some evenings I came home feeling worse, not better. It didn't mean that I didn't still care intensely about my ex-boyfriend. But at least I was out in the world, meeting new people, trying new things. There are only so many hours you can spend ruminating over the past, blaming yourself, wishing that a relationship had turned out differently. That's the thing about life: you can't go back. And you never know what's going to happen next.

While I was busy being alone, I met someone. Not a virtual man, an actual man.

We were in The French House: an iconic Soho watering hole and the scene of many an artistic, theatrical or literary debauch. Regular barflies have included Francis Bacon, Lucian Freud and the poet Dylan Thomas (who once left the manuscript of *Under Milk Wood* under his chair).

It was cold and rainy, the night before Valentine's Day. We were both upstairs in The French House's snug bar, sitting with different groups of friends. One of his colleagues had worked with one of my friends and we all got introduced. I noticed T right away: tall, fair and handsome (although fair is so 'not my type'). He smiled at me across the table and we got talking. Before we left, he asked for my number. The next day he rang me, and the following evening we went out for dinner. And the rest is history.

Looking back now at my dating experiences, I realise that it wasn't until I let go of the past, that my eyes – and my heart – were able to see the possibilities around me. Until I had done some hurting and healing – with a lot of bad dates in between – I wasn't ready to meet anyone new.

I certainly can't pretend I miss Internet dating. But whatever I felt at the time, those wasted evenings weren't wasted at all. The men I met online may not have been right for me, but they were right for another woman. All those preconceptions turned out to be wrong too: they weren't rejects or oddballs, commitment-phobes or philanderers. Things hadn't worked out for them in previous relationships, that's all. There were reasons why they were single, just as there were reasons why I was single, but it didn't make any of us undateable or undeserving of love. However incompatible we might have been, I respected those men: looking for love isn't easy, whether you're 17 or 70. And I ended up respecting myself too.

In my experience, a few bad relationships, broken hearts and 'fallow' periods are no bad thing. Learning to be alone, and to enjoy your own company, makes you more interesting, less emotionally demanding and more able to give to others. We need to believe that we're OK, with or without the status of 'girlfriend', 'boyfriend' or 'other half'. We also need to stop blaming ourselves when things go wrong.

When we let go of the desperate search to find someone who will complete us, we realise something wonderful. We are whole, just the way we are.

Chapter Twelve

A WOUNDED HEALER

Do you know the legend of the Fisher King? According to Arthurian legend, the King charged with guarding the Holy Grail sustains a serious wound, and is unable to heal. Versions of the myth vary, but the wound is usually in the upper thigh or groin, the area of the body that represents masculine fertility. He is effectively impotent and unable to father subsequent generations. Gradually the surrounding lands become as barren as the monarch himself: his kingdom becomes a wasteland. He is unable to do anything but sit beside the river and fish – hence the title Fisher King. Knights travel from far and wide to try to cure him, but only the chosen one will be able to accomplish the feat. Finally, Percival – the chosen one – succeeds in restoring the old man to health. When the Fisher King is healed, his lands become fertile once more.

There are many interpretations of this legend, often focusing on the implications of male impotence – in medieval times, the upper thigh or groin was a euphemism for the male genitalia. The Fisher King's wound is also a powerful metaphor for the way an affliction can spread, infecting everything and everyone around it.

But I take something slightly different from this story. I believe it's the experience of being wounded and then healed that carries significance; it is the wound that enables one to heal, or at least help, others. Most healers begin their journey with mental or physical illness, injury, addiction or emotional trauma. The process of recovery – the journey that leads them from illness to health – is what gives them insight into themselves, and how people heal.

Wounded healer was a term used by the psychotherapist Carl Jung in the early twentieth century to describe how an analyst is drawn to heal others because he himself is wounded. In any therapeutic practice, and in life, healing requires us to acknowledge old wounds and hurts before we can start to mend. Shamanic traditions speak of 'soul loss' and 'soul retrieval': the process by which we begin to heal; retrieving the scattered elements when our soul has been shattered through trauma. When our lives fall apart, we must try to 'pick up the pieces'.

In his book on the Fisher King, the American psychologist Robert Johnson asserts that: 'A healed person is automatically a healer. And his or her strength is the greater for having been through dark times...' This rings very true. For me, helping others has been part of helping myself. The experience of 'dark times' is often more important than the outcome. You don't need to be perfect, or perfectly healed, in order to heal others. The journey itself can be enough.

I'm curious about the process of healing. Whatever our physical, emotional or psychological challenge, where do we find the strength to recover? Is it an individual battle, or can it be shared? Most of the time, one person can't actually heal another – the courage to change has to come from within. But how do we inspire that courage in strangers?

Personally I've been helped by the words of others – from Gerard Manley Hopkins to C. S. Lewis to Naomi Wolf, and many more. Read Hopkins' *Terrible Sonnets*, or Lewis' *A Grief Observed*, or Wolf's *The Beauty Myth*, and you'll see what I mean. Look at the teachings of Julian of Norwich in the fourteenth century, or Nora Ephron in the twenty-first century. Whether it's talking to others, reading books or poetry, words are an incredible solace. They may not solve anything, but they do remind us that we're not alone.

So how and why does it help, sharing our stories? How do we heal each other?

At a recent literary festival, the organisers arranged a book signing after my talk. Every author's nightmare – that no one will turn up – didn't come to pass and fortunately a decent queue of audience members formed. As I signed books, I got the chance to speak to some of the readers. Everyone I met had their own story of dark times, some still struggling, others now free of their eating disorder. It was a surprise to look up and see a little girl standing there, holding a battered copy of *An Apple a Day* for me to sign.

In fact, she was sixteen – but the youngest-looking sixteen year old I've ever met. After I signed her book, she presented me with a gift: a large poster 'to put in your study, when you're writing'. It was a beautiful collage of fruit, vegetables, cut-outs of suns, moons and stars, inspirational quotes, bicycles, bottles of champagne – she must have spent days on it.

She had also written me a long letter, from which I quote (with her permission): 'I just want to thank you for everything you do, it's inspirational and you make me feel like I'm not alone. When I feel down at school I take out your book and feel so much more confident in recovery…'

After I'd signed her book and she'd taken a selfie of the two of us, a man stepped forward and said 'I'm Sarah's father'. He was no more than 40 or 45, but his eyes looked much older. In a low voice he told me that his daughter had been ill with anorexia now for five years, and that he and his wife were absolutely desperate. 'Is there anything – anything at all – we can do to help her get better?' he asked. I said the only thing one can say, which was to keep supporting her and encouraging her, and being there for her. But for the rest of the day I thought about that man's haunted expression. I remember seeing it on my own father's face when I was ill.

Later, on the train back to London, I re-read that young girl's letter and found myself close to tears. I had heard this kind of thing before but I don't think I'd ever taken it in. For the first time it hit me, someone saying: 'You make me feel like I'm not alone.'

Loneliness is one of the worst experiences any of us can go through, and human connection is one of the most precious. I hadn't expected my writing to inspire anyone in that way. Sure, I wanted to reach out to others with anorexia, to encourage them to start eating again, and to demystify the illness for others. But it's overwhelming, to be told by a stranger that you have eased their loneliness, even contributed to their recovery.

In fact, that girl's letter showed just how strong she was. She was so young and yet she had found the strength to fight a life-threatening illness. I'm not exaggerating when I call it life-threatening: anorexia is the most deadly of all mental illnesses:

20 per cent of sufferers will die, from physical complications or suicide. Other estimates put the death toll even higher: a psychiatrist once told me that one third of people with anorexia will die, one third live with the illness for the rest of their life – and only one third recover fully. As modern medicine goes, that is a shockingly high mortality rate.

I have close contact with many of my readers, and I regard that as a privilege. Writing can be a lonely and frustrating business, but when people put their trust in you, when they share their hopes and fears, it makes it all worthwhile. Here are some other tweets I received that week:

> **Bethany Whittaker** @BethanyWhitts When I was in hospital it was you and your book that taught me I can recover from anorexia, you saved my life and I'm so grateful. I'll always look up to you x

> **Lou** @LouisaHemmings @EJWoolf Your writing & support helped me recover from anorexia and saved my life! You're a true hero; keep strong xx

> **Gemma Phazey** @gemmaEphazey @EJWoolf helped me battle through one of the hardest times of my life. Your book gets me through the darkest days & gives me hope :-)

Let me explain. Say you have an eating disorder like anorexia – you've probably been hiding the condition for a long time. After months or years, you face your demons, with or without therapy, and you admit you're ill. Eventually, you decide that you want to recover. But this is only half the battle. Once you start to eat again, once you begin to gain weight, it's unbelievably stressful. Having gone from absolute control over every calorie that passes your lips, now you must double, maybe even triple, that amount. You're forcing yourself to consume 'unsafe' substances like butter, oil, nuts. Every mouthful takes a colossal effort. You can't believe that other people eat *three meals a day, every day*. All you understand is hunger; now you're constantly full. In your rigid anorexic mindset, not being underweight equates to being overweight. Not being hungry equates to greed. Giving up an eating disorder is frightening. It is almost impossible to imagine that the process will ever be OK.

And so, the reason *An Apple a Day* helps those readers is simple: it documents the hellish process of getting back to a healthy weight. Whatever we're going through – whether it's an eating disorder, or another form of addiction, depression, illness or a good old-fashioned broken heart – we desperately need that reassurance, that contrary to how it feels, we're *not* alone.

As an industry, 'self-help' has been booming for several decades. Now, the way we consume our 'self-help' is changing. No longer do we want to be lectured to by old-school experts, usually male, usually American, usually a million miles from where we're at. It's all very well to be told 'men are from Mars, women are from Venus' or to read chapters of advice from a relationship counsellor – but how much more powerful to read about their own relationship breakdown, and eventual recovery. The new self-help gurus are more than experts, they're closer to role models. Increasingly, we respect those who stand up and speak their truth. This new form of truth-speaking depends on a raw kind of honesty.

They're not necessarily saying anything new – self-help advice is basically the same as it's always been: 'Respect yourself, listen to your feelings, make sure you sleep and eat well, connect with others, time will heal.' And of course, overcoming personal problems is the traditional route to helping others in the same predicament. From John Bird, founder of the homeless newspaper *The Big Issue*, who spent many years sleeping rough himself, to 12-step counsellors who have beaten their own alcohol or drug addictions, many people who help others have hit their own rock bottom and recovered. We want to identify with those we take advice from. Beating one's own demons, sharing that journey, inspires others.

Perhaps it's the informality and authenticity that is refreshing. Millennials, Generation Y, the 'we' generation – those in their teens and 20s – are fluent in therapy speak. My teenage students talk quite openly about their 'issues', ranging from emotional abandonment to body dysmorphia to social anxiety disorder. They idolise celebrities like the Olsen twins, Demi Lovato and Taylor Swift precisely because of their public trials and tribulations; 'It makes them relatable,' one student tells me. At their age, I don't think I had any insight into my potential issues, let alone the confidence to discuss them out loud.

Some call it over-sharing and cringe at our warts-and-all confessionalism. It's certainly a world away from the traditional, stiff-upper-lip approach of older generations. For those who lived through world wars, or experienced rationing or material hardship, I'm sure we seem incredibly pampered and soft. For those more used to repression, denial, or just getting on with it, the new truth-speaking can appear self-absorbed, even self-indulgent. But honest sharing can be a valuable reminder that we're not alone.

Social media is the perfect platform for connecting with others, and the new self-help gurus don't hold back. Tweeting, blogging and posting pictures of their daily life, thoughts and meals means that we feel close to them. Sharing our lives online is what we do every day and it's what we expect from our role models. We welcome these daily bursts of inspiration delivered via our smartphones, more immediate and 'relatable' than books, columns or self-help groups.

One of the hippest of self-helpers is Mastin Kipp @ TheDailyLove. A former music producer and drug addict turned blogger, Kipp has more than half a million Twitter followers. He started tweeting about his recovery from addiction and being fired from a top Hollywood music company, and now inspires others. His tweets tend to be funny and uplifting – a recent sample tweet: 'A BREAK-UP is an opportunity to TRADE-UP! Replace the good with the OUTSTANDING!' But it's not all upbeat – Kipp recently blogged about having had 'a really, really s**tty week'. Our gurus are real people, not perfect people; they have failed and been dumped and got addicted. The fact that they're candid about their worst moments, and still got through, gives us hope.

I don't know if I believe that old cliché, 'What doesn't kill you makes you stronger' but I do believe that bad times knock the corners off us. They make us kinder, more patient and more grateful for the good times. Once you've experienced real desolation or pain, you never forget it, and you're never the same person again. Tough situations build strong people; when we're struggling, that's when we're growing and learning. No one would choose to suffer, of course, but it helps to believe that something positive comes from every negative.

Anyway, why bother pretending? Life is random, sometimes unbearably cruel: illness, tragedy or disaster can strike at any time. The truth is that none of us is unscathed by life or perfectly whole. We bear our bruises and scars in different places, and we cope in different ways.

'So are you fully recovered now?' This question has followed me around since I wrote *An Apple a Day*, and I still don't have the answer.

First, what does 'recovered' actually mean? Is an alcoholic who hasn't drunk alcohol for six weeks recovered? Probably not. Six months? Or six years? How do we know that the alcoholism isn't still inside? There are no guarantees: all we can do is live each day as fully as possible, and that's a healthy life. Second, what are these labels anyway? How do we define ourselves? I'm a sister and a daughter. I'm a writer and a journalist. I'm not a wife or mother. I'm not an anorexic.

If recovery means a healthy weight, then yes I'm recovered. Are there still foods I avoid? Yes. Would I ever avoid a special meal out with friends? No. Do I ever think about my weight? Sure. But I don't weigh myself, I don't hate my body or have 'fat days' – and I don't let my feelings about food get in the way of living a full life.

I think all of this makes me pretty much normal. We all have the odd hang-up about our bodies these days, male or female, young or old, and many of us have dietary quirks or unusual eating habits. Accepting that nothing is perfect, that progress can be up and down, has been part of the recovery itself. I have learned to worry less, even to appreciate uncertainty. It was the Romantic poet John Keats who invented the concept of 'negative capability': 'When a man is capable of being in uncertainties, mysteries, doubts, without any irritable reaching after fact and reason.' I feared uncertainty for a long time. Now I welcome the unpredictability of life, the fact that one never knows what's around the next corner.

And it's exhilarating, after years of lying about the food I'd supposedly eaten and the hunger I claimed not to feel, to be completely open. I finally confessed the thing I'd been most ashamed about – and you know what? The sky didn't fall in. People didn't laugh at me; in fact they told me they had similar issues, or knew someone who did. When you take that terrifying leap, when you admit you have a problem and start to accept help, it gives you a rush, a sort of drunken confidence... *Wait, I can do* this, *the thing which petrifies me, and actually it's OK?*

I try to hang on to that confidence when I have dark moments, to remember that change is always possible. Things were bad for many years, but slowly they got better. I can't think of many positives to those years of isolation and hunger. But recovery has taught me to be honest and to believe in myself. So is Robert Johnson right – are all healed people automatically healers? Are we really stronger in the broken places? Sometimes what doesn't kill you, just doesn't kill you. Sometimes the wound isn't where the light gets in, but just scar tissue. And sometimes we're just treading water. Looking back, it seems like I spent years just surviving each day. It felt pointless, it felt futile – but was it a waste of life? I often read these lines from *Kafka on the Shore* by Haruki Murakami: 'When you come out of the storm, you won't be the same person who walked in. That's what this storm's all about.'

Getting through the storm is an achievement in itself. I believe that no matter how bad things get, there is always hope. You must not give up. I did not give up. And that is not nothing.

I recently received an email from a woman who had just read my book, *The Ministry of Thin*. She told me she had spent her entire life hating her appearance. Now, aged 37, she was getting married and had just bought her first bikini: 'Although I'm not 100 per cent happy with my body, I do feel that I can now wear a bikini on my honeymoon without feeling mortified that I'm not perfect.'

It was that lovely detail about the bikini that moved me, knowing that woman would be on her honeymoon with a tiny bit more body confidence. Surely that's what it means to be human: sharing our imperfect, honest experiences and recognising each other for the imperfect, beautiful creatures we are.

Sharing with others really does help. Unspoken hurt festers. There is evidence that shame is corrosive and keeping secrets harms us. Whether the trauma is great or small, it invariably gets worse when it's locked up inside. In her book *Daring Greatly*, Brené Brown cites research carried out by Professor James Pennebaker at the University of Texas: 'The act of not discussing a traumatic event or confiding it to another person could be more damaging than the actual event. Conversely, when people shared their stories and experiences, their physical health improved, their doctor's visits decreased, and they showed significant decreases in their stress hormones.'

Trauma is a frightening word – like me, you may not feel your problems classify as 'traumatic'. For years I would minimise what I was going through, starting every consultation with a new psychiatrist: 'I have nothing to complain about, my life is privileged, I'm lucky really...' Well, I *was* lucky and all that, but obviously something was still very wrong. Whatever the challenge you're facing, if it matters, it matters.

This doesn't mean you have to divulge your deepest feelings with everyone, or publicly over-share. It doesn't mean that you have to be part of a fabulous *Girls* or *Sex and the City*-style group of friends either; some of us are fine with solitude (I love being alone). But talking to others can be immensely healing. Emotional isolation is terrible: panic, sickness or fear, the feeling that no one else has ever been where we are, alone with our despair. As the sociologists Miller and Stiver at Wellesley College in Massachusetts, write: '... the most terrifying and destructive feeling that a person can experience is psychological isolation. This is not the same as being alone. It is a feeling of being locked out of the possibility of human connection.'

Human beings are, essentially, social beings. We may think we don't need others, but we do. At lonely moments I've often found myself lifted by a few cheery words from the lady behind the till at the supermarket. Someone calling me 'duckie' or commenting on the weather. Whether it's with a friend, stranger or sibling, whether it's a smile, a tweet or a hug, human interaction matters. If you do find yourself feeling isolated from the world around you, remember that you're not alone. There are telephone and Internet helplines available if you need to talk to someone urgently; there are forums, chat rooms and meet-up groups. Meeting up with others may be the last thing you feel like doing, but it really helps.

Sometimes other people *won't* understand what you're going through: sometimes they can't. My father, for example, was an incredible source of love and support when I was anorexic – but how could he understand this strange compulsion to not eat?

Similarly, healing others doesn't always mean solving their problems: sometimes there is no solution. My friend Tamsin telling me about the horrendous divorce she had been through years before didn't mend my heartbreak, but it reminded me that I would survive. Knowing that others have survived what you're going through makes the world of difference. It's healing just to know you're not alone.

One of the most inspiring contemporary examples of this is the TV presenter and campaigner Katie Piper. In March 2008, an ex-boyfriend arranged to have her attacked in the street, with sulphuric acid thrown in her face. The acid melted away her left ear and eyelids, damaged her lungs, throat, arms, hands and neck, and blinded her in one eye. Surgeons had to remove all the skin from her face before rebuilding it. In the intervening years she has undergone more than 200 corrective operations, including countless skin grafts and other major surgery.

Before the attack she was a stunningly pretty, up-and-coming young model; now she has built something equally beautiful out of her tragedy. Not only did she set up her own charity, the Katie Piper Foundation, which offers medical and psychological support to victims of disfigurement, but she has become an inspiration to thousands. Her books *Beautiful*, and *Things Get Better*, are uplifting for anyone going through tough times. Like all the best books, they touch something universal in their readers.

Until recently, Katie also wrote an advice column for *Now* magazine. I happened to pick up a copy in the hairdresser's and read her final column. These words resonated with me: 'We never know what someone's going through just by looking at them. We can be envious of people online, but away from the seemingly "perfect" photos and status updates, we're all muddling through life the best we can.' Next to her column was a photo of her lying in her hospital bed, soon after the acid attack, gravely injured. She writes: 'Knowing I'm not the only one with scars is so reassuring. Lots of us have scars – they're just not always visible.'

Katie Piper waived her right to anonymity, and her whole life has changed. Wherever she goes strangers want to tell her of their own struggles. As she says: 'There's no day off once you've gone out there and spoken about that. People come up and talk about the worst things that have ever happened... You don't know whether they've been raped or attacked or have burns under their clothes.' In speaking about the attack, giving up her privacy and showing the world her scars, she has given hope to many others. She is a wounded healer of the most amazing kind.

I don't compare my journey with Katie's: she has faced far greater challenges and hers were not self-inflicted. In the end, I'm not a healer or a role model. All I have done is what others have done for me, which is to share my personal story. Now, when someone tells me 'you saved my life' I don't dismiss it as exaggeration – because I've been 'saved' at times too. Perhaps it is that simple: we help by sharing, listening and being there. No one is only wounded, or only a healer. We are strong and weak in different places. We all heal each other.

Conclusion

No attempt to let go will ever be perfect. We can't let go of everything, nor should we try to: our past experiences, good and bad, are as much a part of us as our future plans. But when we're stuck, when we find we're hurting ourselves, or holding ourselves back, this is when we need to work on letting go. What I have tried to do in this book is to look at what Henry James called 'the things that help with the things that hurt'.

We all fail and fall at times; we make mistakes and blame ourselves; we fall in love with the wrong people for the wrong reasons, and we experience guilt and envy and low self-worth. The business of being human can be messy, embarrassing, even downright painful. But sometimes things have to go very wrong before they can come right. Going through bad times is what makes the good times feel so good. Life is all about contrasts: think of how delicious food tastes when you're very hungry, or what a relief it is to rest after intense exercise. If success and joy were guaranteed, they would not feel half so precious. I strongly believe that when we survive loss or sadness of any kind, we emerge as kinder and wiser people, with a greater capacity for love. I have seen this in my own life and in the lives of others.

Letting go doesn't mean that we disengage from emotions, that we never expose our deepest feeling, never risk our hearts, or that we keep ourselves safe and distant and detached. By its very nature, being open makes us vulnerable. As we've seen, letting go isn't about giving up either. It's not about ignoring or repressing pain, or pretending that bad things haven't happened. (Show me the person who hasn't been bruised by life.)

Letting go is braver than that. It's refusing to allow our past to define our present or future. It's recognising when we're holding ourselves back with *if onlys* and *what ifs*. It's taking action when we're clinging to unhappy memories or unhelpful neuroses, trapped by damaging habits or addictions, sabotaging our true potential. We save ourselves a great deal of angst when we decide to leave the past where it belongs: behind us. No matter how impossible it seems, we just need to let it go.

When I find myself struggling, I remind myself of these words from Buddha: 'No one saves us but ourselves. No one can and no one may. We ourselves must walk the path.' Friends, family or therapists can provide advice and support, but in the end it comes down to you as an individual making that choice to keep trying, no matter what. Surround yourself with kind people, by all means, and treat others well. But remember that no one else's love and care can replace you loving and caring for yourself. We all go wrong sometimes, we get hurt and hurt others. But we also have the capacity to start afresh, every morning if need be. Belief in oneself, compassion for others, and a generous helping of optimism, can work wonders. When things seem hopeless, when there's nothing to look forward to, make something up – write a list, formulate a plan, work towards a dream, plan a journey, start a conversation. Invent your reason to keep going.

And don't ever think you're alone, because you're not. The sooner you can rid yourself of the notion that everyone else is 'sorted', the better. In fact, others are usually kinder, less confident, and more vulnerable than you might think. We all feel lost at times, we all feel alone and we all struggle.

Of course it's not easy. Growth is painful. Change is painful. Giving up on a dream or a relationship, forgiving and forgetting, saying goodbye, laying ghosts to rest, all that can hurt like crazy. But nothing is as painful as staying stuck in a bad place. I remember someone once said to me, 'We have only moments to live.' It's true, isn't it: moments are all we have. Let's make every moment matter: let's risk being happy.

Letting go can be transformative. For me, it's been truly liberating. When you decide to let go of slights or resentments, anxiety over status or salary, your body or the bathroom scales, when you stop comparing yourself and worrying what others think – when you let go of all the stuff that *doesn't* matter, quite simply you're left with what *does*. Letting go is the first step towards changing your life. Don't hold on... let go.

FURTHER READING

FURTHER READING

Brown, Brené *Daring Greatly: How the Courage to Be Vulnerable Transforms the Way We Live, Love, Parent, and Lead* (2012, Gotham Books)

de Beauvoir, Simone *The Second Sex* (1953, Jonathan Cape)

Gilbert, Elizabeth *Eat, Pray, Love: One Woman's Search for Everything* (2006, Bloomsbury)

Hesse, Hermann *Siddhartha* (1954, Peter Owen)

Jeffers, Susan *Feel the Fear and Do It Anyway* (1987, Century)

Kabat-Zinn, Jon *Full Catastrophe Living: How to cope with stress, pain and illness using mindfulness meditation* (1996, Piatkus)

Orbach, Susie *Hunger Strike* (1986, Faber and Faber)

Sandberg, Sheryl *Lean In: Women, Work, and the Will to Lead* (2013, Alfred A. Knopf)

Sisson, Mark *The Primal Blueprint* (2009, Primal Nutrition)

Tolle, Eckhart *The Power of Now* (2005, Hodder Mobius)

Wilde, Oscar *De Profundis* (1986, Penguin Classics)

Woolf, Emma *An Apple a Day: A Memoir of Love and Recovery from Anorexia* (2012, Summersdale Publishers)

Woolf, Emma *The Ministry of Thin: How the Pursuit of Perfection Got Out of Control* (2013, Summersdale Publishers)

RESOURCES

Anorexia and Bulimia Care
www.anorexiabulimiacare.org.uk

Beat
www.b-eat.co.uk

Brainworks
www.brainworksneurotherapy.com

Depression Alliance
www.depressionalliance.org

Emma Woolf's website
www.emmawoolf.com

Men Get Eating Disorders Too
www.mengetedstoo.co.uk

Mental Health Foundation
www.mentalhealth.org.uk

Mind
www.mind.org.uk

National Centre for Eating Disorders
www.eating-disorders.org.uk

NHS
www.nhs.uk

Samaritans
www.samaritans.org

Sane
www.sane.org.uk

Transformational Retreats
www.transformational-retreats.com

UK Feminista
www.ukfeminista.org.uk

The Vagenda
www.vagendamagazine.com

Have you enjoyed this book?
If so, why not write a review on your favourite website?

If you're interested in finding out more about our books, find us on Facebook at **Summersdale Publishers** and follow us on Twitter at **@Summersdale**.

Thanks very much for buying this Summersdale book.
www.summersdale.com